GUNS AT SEA
The World's Great Naval Battles

GUNS AT SEA
The World's Great Naval Battles

Len Ortzen

Foreword by Ludovic Kennedy

Galahad Books New York City

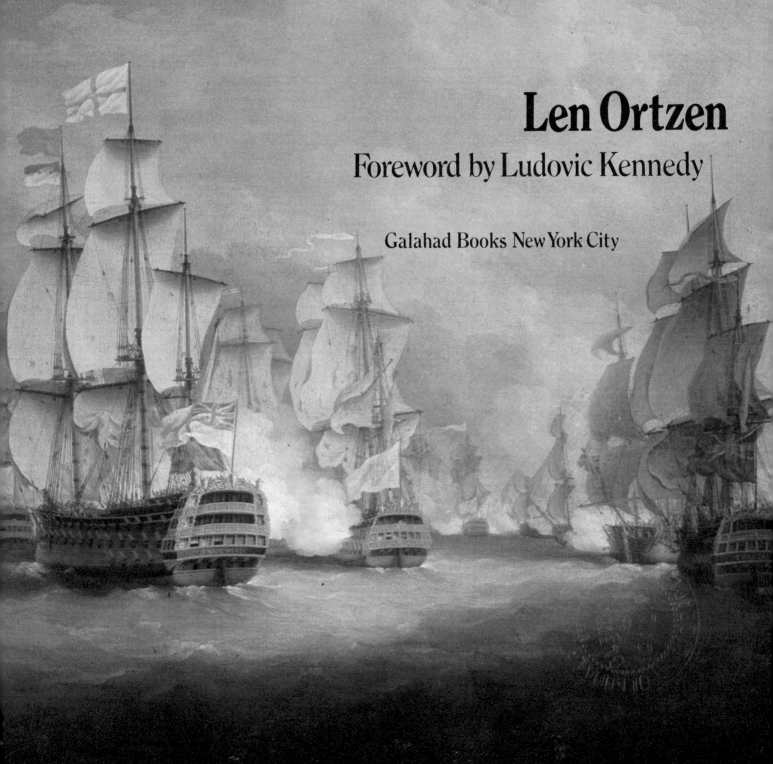

12/77

CONTENTS

Foreword by Ludovic Kennedy   7

1 'Murderous and Horrible'   9
   The Battle of Sluys, 1340

2 The Crescent sinks in the East   15
   Lepanto, 1571

3 'The most fortunate fleet'   28
   The Spanish Armada, 1588

4 America's First Naval Hero   40
   Flamborough Head, 1779

5 Far-reaching Consequences   47
   Chesapeake Bay, 1781

6 Mutinous but Victorious   52
   Cape St Vincent, 1797

7 The Nelson Touch   59
   Trafalgar, 1805

8 The last Battle fought under Sail   75
   Navarino, 1827

9 The Coming of the Ironclads   83
   Hampton Roads, 1862

10 An American Duel at Dawn   89
   Cherbourg, 1864

11 The Russians' Long Haul to Disaster   94
   Tsushima, 1905

12 Where the Germans Deserved Better   105
   The Falklands, 1914

13 A Classic Naval Battle   115
   The Drama of the Graf Spee, *1939*

14 A Very Close-run Thing   125
   Sinking the Bismarck, *1941*

15 The Japs have it all their Own Way   137
   Java Sea, 1942

16 The Beginning of the End   146
   Midway, 1942

Further Reading   156
Acknowledgments   157
Index   158

Foreword

by Ludovic Kennedy

Most people think of sea-battles as exciting but isolated events; and yet, as history shows, their effects have often reached far beyond the immediate outcome of the battle. The defeat of the French at Sluys opened the way to the Hundred Years War; Chesapeake Bay determined the course of the American War of Independence; the sinking of the Bismarck and the battle of Midway showed that sea-power without air-power was nothing. Trafalgar did not lead directly to the defeat of Napoleon, nor Jutland to that of the Kaiser, yet the loss of the first would have meant a French invasion of England, and the second the German fleet starving us into surrender. As Churchill said of Admiral Jellicoe, the Grand Fleet's commander: 'He is the only man on either side who can lose the war in an afternoon'.

In the old days sea-battles were fought like land battles, only at sea. With ships locked together by grappling irons, soldiers – specially embarked for the purpose – swarmed over the sides to attack each other with swords and pikes in bloody hand-to-hand fighting. With the invention of the muzzle-loaded cannon ships fought at a distance – though never so far that their crews could not clearly see each other – and captains kept speaking-trumpets handy to inquire if their opponents were ready to strike. In the twentieth century came high explosive which increased gun range to fifteen miles. At Jutland, where more than 8,000 men were killed, neither side ever saw the faces of their enemies.

Most sea-battles are cleaner, nobler affairs than battles on land – no refugees or spies, no houses, roads, cattle, crops, to muddy the terrain. Warships combine uniquely elegance and power; and their names, often commemorating heroes of their country's past (Marlborough, Scharnhorst, Richelieu, Washington, Cavour), bestow an added dignity and grace. Sailors too have an affinity with their enemies that soldiers lack; for a ship is a sailor's home, and so to be cherished for itself. Those of us who saw *Bismarck* die felt not just relief that she was now out of the way, but awe that so fine a piece of craftsmanship should be reduced to such a wreck, pity for those still inside. *Bismarck*'s crew when they blew up the *Hood*, felt the same.

Will there ever be sea-battles again, as Len Ortzen has described them so vividly in his book, or has the threat of all-out atomic war made them obsolete? All one can say at present is that the Soviet Navy has grown and continues to grow in strength and numbers, and that while we know its capabilities, we have no guide as to its intentions. Certainly, if there ever is another naval war, it will be like no other, with ships in combat over the horizon, submarines destroying each other at vast depths, nuclear missiles and torpedoes obliterating convoys at a stroke. In comparison Lepanto and Tsushima and Jutland will seem quite homely affairs.

1 'Murderous and Horrible'

The Battle of Sluys, 1340

Before guns were mounted in ships, fighting at sea was little different from fighting on land. Opposing ships sought only to get to close quarters as soon as possible; 'grapple and board' was the order of the day. This frequently led to ferocious hand-to-hand fighting and scenes of carnage. Perhaps none more so in medieval times than at the Battle of Sluys, called by Jean Froissart, the French chronicler, 'that murderous and horrible battle'.

The cause of this confrontation was the claim of Edward III of England to the French crown. He was a grandson of Philippe IV through his mother; French lawyers had not then invented the Salic law forbidding succession through a female, but the nobles preferred a Frenchman for their monarch and crowned Philippe of Valois (Philippe VI), a nephew of Philippe IV. Edward persisted in his claim, and war between the two became inevitable. The quarrel was envenomed by French interference with the Anglo-Flemish wool trade.

Each king began assembling all the ships he could lay hands on, in order to carry his knights and men-at-arms to wage war on the other. It was a long business. France did not even have an admiral. The man appointed, Hue Quiéret, was ordered to assemble a fleet of transports for Philippe's 'Grand Army of the Sea'.

By the spring of 1340 there were nearly two hundred ships ready in French Channel ports. The crews had been recruited chiefly from local fishermen; the archers and men-at-arms came principally from Picardy and Normandy. One hundred and fifty knights and barons had joined the expedition, bringing four hundred crossbowmen with them. The only experienced seamen were the crews of the royal galleys and of four Genoese galleys, the latter led by a wily sea-captain named Barbavera, who had hired them out to the French king. This force of some two hundred vessels and more than twenty thousand men sailed from Boulogne and Calais and moved slowly up the coast, waiting for a favourable wind to cross to the Thames estuary. On 8 June they were off the mouth of the Scheldt, and Admiral Quiéret decided to anchor there.

Edward III had been having as much difficulty as the French king in assembling a fleet, and was ready at about the same time. Two hundred vessels of all sizes were mustered on the East Coast of England, and in June the army began to embark – knights in full armour and with squires leading their sturdy warhorses, pikemen, light infantry armed with longbows. News had been received that the French were concentrating their forces off the coast of Flanders, and early in the morning of 22 June Edward's mixed armada got under way.

The weather was set fair, with a rising breeze from the northeast – perfect conditions for a swift passage to Flanders. The Royal standard bearing the lilies of France in support of Edward's claim to be 'King of England and of France' was flown in the great ship *Thomas*, which had aboard the leading

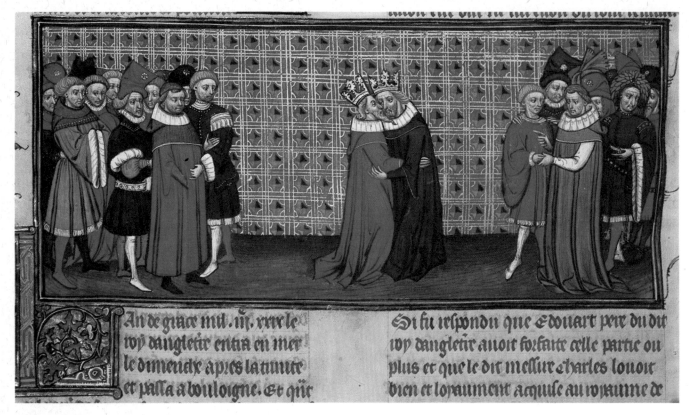

An de grace mil .iij. xxix le
roy dangleisr entra en mer
le dimenche apres la trinite
et passa a boulloigne. Et qui

Si fu respondu que Edouart pere du dit
roy dangleisr auoit forfaitte celle partie ou
plus et que le dit messur charles louoit
bien et loyaument acquise au royaume de

ABOVE Edward III paying homage
to Philippe VI in 1329. In eight
years they were at war.

names of English chivalry. The fleet made a brave and gay display with
all the many-coloured banners and pennants fluttering in the breeze. One
gilded and painted ship was carrying some ladies of the Court, to be present
at the battle as at a tournament and distribute favours to the victors – the
English of course.

At midday on the twenty-third the fleet made its landfall. 'The dunes of
Blankenbergh,' cried the lookout in the *Thomas*. The king decided to
anchor there for the night. The smaller ships were hauled up the beach, and
the soldiers bivouacked ashore to recover from the crossing. Some Flemish
fishermen came hurrying with the news that the French were moored in the
Scheldt estuary a few miles to the east. Instead of sending a fast-sailing vessel
to reconnoitre, it was thought better to use some of the horses as they had
suffered badly from seasickness and would be happy to stretch their legs.
So a party of knights went cantering across the dunes towards the town of
Sluys and the Scheldt.

It was in fact a wise decision. This naval reconnaissance by cavalry was
able to note the disposition and strength of the enemy better from land than a
vessel could have done from seaward. Quiéret had drawn up his ships in
three divisions, one behind the other, in front of the town of Sluys. Their
prows were pointing seawards and were lashed together, and had makeshift
wooden barriers across the bows as defence against boarding and to give
shelter to bowmen and soldiers. In short, Quiéret had transformed his naval
force into a floating fort.

Five 'great ships' captured from the English in a raid two years
previously were in advance of the front line. Nearest to attack from the sea
was the *Great Christopher*, commanded by a Flemish sea-captain. Quiéret
was flying his banner in the *St George*, a little to the rear.

Alone of the French fleet, Barbavera, who had stressed the folly of waiting

·CCC· iiij· viij·

J toft que ces agfou
fuient deuant les

fuient ce premier io. tonant
lancant escarmouchit et

on the defensive, was cruising off the estuary with his galleys. His lookouts had seen the forest of masts and sails to the west, and the Genoese returned with all speed to the *St George*. 'Up anchor and set sail quickly,' he urged Quiéret. 'You're in a cul-de-sac here. At daybreak tomorrow the English will bear down on you; they'll be borne in by the wind, your bowmen will have the sun in their eyes, and you'll be trapped!' But Quiéret would have none of it. 'Shame on any who depart from here!' he cried. Barbavera saw it was useless to insist, but resolved not to be trapped himself.

When Edward III received the report on the enemy's dispositions from the little force of cavalry he decided to attack the following morning, 24 June, the Feast of St John.

At five that morning the tide was just on the turn, and the English ships drew off on the ebb. The fleet began to scud before the wind for the river mouth. Two ships crashed into the bows and the port side of the

ABOVE Sea warfare was to change little during the Hundred Years War that followed the battle of Sluys – a naval battle off La Rochelle in 1372, from Froissart's Chronicles.

11

RIGHT The English fleet, from the late fourteenth-century *Chroniques d'Angleterre* by Jean Wavrin.

OPPOSITE 'Grapple and board', a fourteenth-century battle at sea.

Christopher, and, with a cry of 'St George for England!', a score of knights vied with each other for the honour of being the first to board the enemy.

The other ships of the English van swung in bow to bow, threw out their grapples and fought furiously to gain an entry. With sword and pike, and a deluge of missiles from the fighting-tops, the French fought to thrust back the invaders. Back and forth swayed the tussle; Edward was in the forefront of the fray, wielding his gleaming sword. The French second-in-command, Nicolas Béhuchet, sought out the English king and succeeded in wounding him in the thigh.

As Barbavera had foreseen, Quiéret's dispositions prevented the ships in the second and third lines from aiding the first, on which the English attack was concentrated. Ship after ship was cleared from the left inward. The English archers were discharging their arrows at thrice the speed of the enemy, and the French losses were visibly mounting. Quarter was neither asked nor given; each captured ship was cleared of its crew, dead and

wounded alike being tossed overboard. After several hours of fierce fighting, the five great ships were again in English hands. Quiéret, badly wounded, was captured and beheaded; and Béhuchet, attacked by knights enraged at his insult to their king's person, was also taken. A few minutes later his body was swinging from the yard-arm of the *Thomas*. This summary execution had a disastrous effect on the French; they began to give way when they saw that their leaders' banners were no longer flying from the *St George*.

The men in the second and third lines of ships had stoutly resisted the advance of the English until then, although their ranks were thinned by the deadly flights of arrows. A giant Norman, Pierre d'Estelang, standing in the bows of his ship, wielded his sword to such effect that he was said to have slain or wounded more than a hundred of the enemy before being brought down himself. He was left for dead, but in fact survived the fight.

The sun was slipping below the horizon. Dead in their thousands littered the decks. Groups of fighters, linked in fierce hand-to-hand combat, had gone overside together. The waters were running red with blood; and the flames from burning vessels stood out more clearly as night began to fall.

The flames brought local fishermen hurrying for the pickings. They took the hard-pressed French from behind, and panic overcame the remnants of the 'Grand Army of the Sea'. Hundreds of them were drowned while struggling to reach the river banks in the gathering darkness.

Most of the royal galleys succeeded in cutting their moorings and, aided by the ebbing tide, reached the open sea. These vessels, with a few Dieppe barges and other ships, including Barbavera's galleys, were the only ones to escape from the disaster. For days afterwards, wounded survivors were seen trickling back through Flanders 'in rags and much distressed in body'. At the French court there was great consternation. Nobody dared tell King Philippe of the disaster, and eventually it was the court jester who blurted out the news.

Edward III now held command of the Channel and could carry the conflict to French soil at any point he cared to choose. In July 1346 his choice fell on the Cherbourg peninsula. At the head of a great fleet he landed at St Vaast-la-Hougue, burnt the few French vessels in the harbour, razed Cherbourg and Barfleur, and with his greatest barons and some twelve thousand men started on the march eastwards that was to lead to the famous victory at Crécy a month later.

The Hundred Years War had begun.

2 The Crescent sinks in the East

Lepanto, 1571

After the fifteenth century the man-of-war, which had been just a means of troop transport, became more and more a floating gun-platform. Henceforth the fighting prowess of the warship would rest on the guns – their number and weight of shot, their accuracy and rate of fire. Sail power and manœuvrability were important too, though less so in the Mediterranean where the oar-propelled galley, with cannon mounted fore and aft, remained the chief fighting ship until well into the seventeenth century.

By the mid-sixteenth century, however, a few galleasses were coming into service. The galleass was a greatly enlarged galley, bristling with guns, which had its oar-power augmented by three lateen-rigged masts. It was the capital ship of the day. The summit of its achievement was at the Battle of Lepanto, in the Gulf of Patras, in 1571. More than two hundred galleys, galleasses and other vessels from the Catholic countries of the Mediterranean, carrying twenty-eight thousand soldiers, fought an even larger Muslim fleet from morning till dusk on 7 October. Although only six galleasses were present, all in the Christian fleet, their firepower was of great assistance in the early stages of the battle.

The confrontation was in the nature of a later Crusade. Turkish armies had driven a wedge deep into Europe, and Muslim fleets were in command of much of the Mediterranean. In 1570 the Turks invaded Cyprus, a possession of the Republic of Venice, and laid siege to Famagusta, the capital. The aged Pope Pius V succeeded in forming the Holy League, an alliance of the maritime powers of southern Europe against Christendom's common enemy. In the summer of 1571 their forces began to assemble at the appointed rendezvous, Messina, in the straits between Sicily and the toe of Italy. Pius V, exercising his right as chief of the League and all his prestige, had appointed as commander-in-chief Don John of Austria, a natural son of the Emperor Charles V. He was only twenty-four but had already proved himself a bold leader on land and sea. His command consisted of the Spanish Mediterranean fleet, a squadron from the Papal States, squadrons from Genoa and Venice, and three galleys of the Knights of Malta. The largest force was provided by Venice – 107 galleys and all 6 galleasses. The alliance was an uneasy affair, and much tact was required by Don John to unify the fleet and reconcile the different nationalities.

Meanwhile the Turkish fleet was concentrating in the Gulf of Patras, just east of the bay of Lepanto where the gulf narrowed and was protected by a fort on either bank. The commander-in-chief, Ali Pasha, had received news of the Christian armada assembling at Messina and sent one of his best corsairs, an Arab named Kara Khodja, to reconnoitre Sicilian waters. Khodja painted his galley black and one dark night he hoisted black sails and slipped unseen into Messina harbour. Gliding unchallenged about the waters, he counted the vessels, then hastened back to report to Ali Pasha on the strength of the Christian fleet.

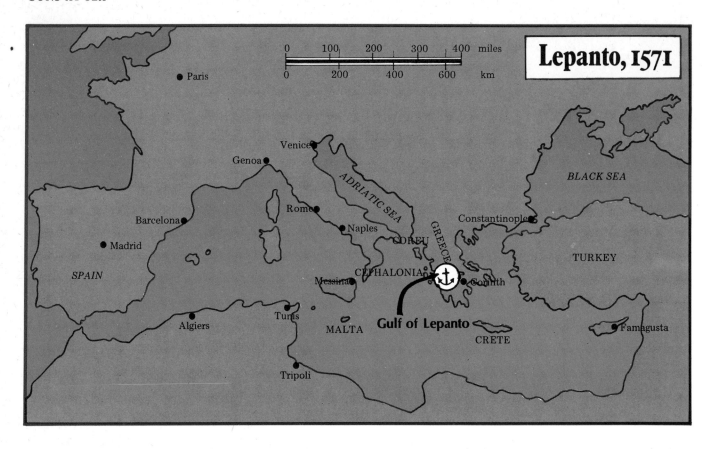

Lepanto, 1571

BELOW The aged Pope Pius V, founder of the Holy League against the 'infidel Turk'.

It was a misleading report, for not all the League's forces had reached the rendezvous. Don John and the important Spanish contingent arrived on 23 August, the commander-in-chief flying his flag in the *Reale*, a magnificent galley which had a crew of three hundred rowers and carried four hundred soldiers.

Don John wisely formed the Christian fleet into five squadrons, each with ships of the different nationalities. He took command of the centre squadron of sixty-two galleys flying blue pennons; the left wing of fifty-three galleys flying yellow pennons was given to Agostino Barbarigo of Venice, brother of the general besieged in Famagusta; the right wing commanded by Andrea Doria of Genoa comprised fifty galleys flying green pennons. Seven swift galleys formed the vanguard under Juan de Cardona of Spain, and the reserve of thirty galleys was held by the Marquis of Santa Cruz.

On 16 September the fleet put to sea, the *Reale* leading, while on shore the Papal envoy gave the blessing of Pius V to the whole enterprise. The course was along the foot and heel of Italy and then to the island of Corfu, a distance of about two hundred miles – less than a day's run for an ordinary ship today. Don John and his fleet took ten days, but this was chiefly due to stormy weather.

The Christian fleet straggled into Corfu harbour, the rowers worn out by head-winds, driving rain and heavy seas, on 26 September. The commandant of the fortress gave news of the fall of Famagusta on 18 August. The starving garrison had capitulated after the Turks had promised to spare their lives and allow them to sail to Crete; but once in the Turks' power the Venetian soldiers had been taken into slavery, their officers beheaded and their general, Bragadino, flayed alive. All this served to strengthen the

LEFT Don John of Austria, commander-in-chief of the Holy League.

resolve of Don John and his officers; although it seemed that, with the fall of Cyprus, the Ottoman fleet would receive reinforcements.

Don John remained four days at Corfu, resting his crews and embarking four thousand troops of the garrison. He sent four fast galleys under the command of Gil d'Andrada to reconnoitre the Turkish fleet; it was thought to be assembled in or near the Gulf of Patras, but it might equally well have put to sea. On 30 September Don John led his fleet south to the island of Cephalonia, opposite the entrance to the Gulf of Patras, where Andrada

OVERLEAF The battle of Lepanto by an unknown artist.

17

ABOVE Andrea Doria of Genoa, the commander of the right wing of fifty galleys flying green pennons.

rejoined with the news that the enemy strength in vessels was less than two hundred and that the crews had been decimated by the plague.

At the same time, Ali Pasha had sent Kara Khodja on another mission to spy out the strength of the Christians. The Arab had found them at Corfu, but the harbour entrance was guarded and he had been unable to approach so closely as at Messina; however, what he saw made him believe that the Christian fleet was no stronger than when he had counted it earlier. Thus it was that each commander-in-chief believed the other to be inferior in strength and consequently hastened to bring him to battle.

The Turks weighed anchor and moved towards the mouth of the Gulf. Their fleet was in fact 274 sail strong, of which 210 were galleys and 44 galliots, the latter almost as large as some of the Christian galleys. All the Turkish craft had sails as well as oars; and twenty-five thousand soldiers, many of them well-trained janissaries, had been embarked in the fleet. The centre squadron of eighty-seven galleys was commanded by Ali Pasha; the right wing composed of fifty-four galleys was under the command of the governor of Alexandria, Mohammed Scirocco, and the left wing of sixty-one galleys and thirty-two galliots was under El Louck Ali, Viceroy of Algiers. It was a formidable display of power, but Ali Pasha's superiority in numbers was offset by several disadvantages: his fighting-men were armed more with bows and arrows than muskets; his galleys had low bulwarks without protective shields; and the twelve thousand or so galley-slaves had nothing to gain from a Turkish victory, whereas defeat would mean liberation from their chains for those who survived the battle.

Meanwhile the Christian fleet lay weather-bound under the lee of the island of Cephalonia. On 6 October the wind shifted to the east and the sea began to go down. Don John refused to wait any longer. The fleet put to sea under oar-power alone, and that night moored off the mainland barely twenty miles from the Muslim fleet at the entrance to the Gulf. Hardly had they got under way again at dawn than the leading galleys sighted the Turkish sails. The signal was sent back, 'Enemy in sight'. It was an anxious time for the Christian admirals. The fleet was strung out, hampered by the head-wind. Fortunately the wind suddenly dropped and the sea fell calm. The Turkish crews were seen to be clewing and furling their now useless sails with a common accord and a rapidity which their enemies could not help admiring. Oars alone now became the motive power for the battle. This slower approach of the Turkish galleys gave the Christians more time to take up their battle stations.

In the *Reale*, Don John had the purple-and-gold standard consecrated by Pius V broken out from the mainmast for the first time. It portrayed Christ crucified, with St Peter and St Paul on either side. Ali Pasha was flying a white standard on which verses from the Koran were inscribed in gold letters.

Don John temporarily left his flagship and embarked in a galley; standing in the bow and holding high a crucifix, he was rowed along the forming line of the fleet. When he returned to the *Reale* a gun was fired as a signal to attack.

Don John sent orders to Barbarigo for the left wing to reach as far inshore as possible, to prevent the Turks outflanking them. As each galley reached her fighting position, the oarsmen were freed and given weapons; unlike the Turks' galley-slaves, these were either men hired for the campaign or convicts sentenced to a term in the galleys, and the latter were promised a pardon

LEFT Agostino Barbarigo of Venice, the commander of the left wing of fifty-three galleys flying yellow pennons.

or remission of part of their sentence in the event of victory.

The sun was high in the sky when the long Turkish line came speeding to the onset. Don John's battle array was still incomplete; Doria's squadron had yet to get into position on the right wing, and the two galleasses with him were well astern, being towed by galleys. However the two galleasses with the centre squadron were well out in front, as were the two on the left. The four big ships belched forth with all their cannon as the Ottoman galleys came sweeping into range, and caused great confusion and much destruction. One of the first shots crashed into the deck of Ali Pasha's flagship. The Turkish line swayed and lost impetus. The cannonade continued, the range closing all the time; but the Turks came on in close formation in spite of the hail of gunshot, and began to grapple and board their enemies.

Barbarigo, on the left wing, sustained the first attack from Mohammed Scirocco in a great Alexandrian galley, while some Turkish galleys managed to slip inshore, as Don John had feared, and take Barbarigo in the rear. The janissaries fought like demons, boarding Barbarigo's galley and clearing

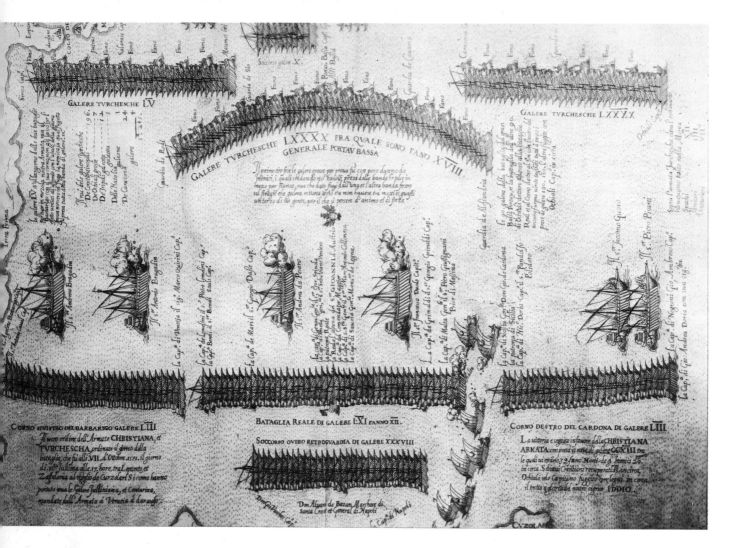

A contemporary engraving showing the disposition of the Turkish and Christian fleets, the numbers of ships involved and the names of the commanders.

the deck as far as the mainmast. Barbarigo was wounded, and the situation was becoming desperate. Then a rush of Venetians and Spaniards from the next galleys drove the boarders from the deck of the flagship. After fierce hand-to-hand fighting in which Scirocco was killed, the Alexandrian galley was captured. The Egyptian standard was hauled down, the Christian galley-slaves were freed and the Muslim prisoners were chained to the benches in their place. This success seemed to make victory certain on the Christians' left wing. The Turks there began to lose confidence, and some beached their galleys or started to withdraw up the Gulf.

In the centre, matters were not going so well for the Christians. The galleasses had to hold their fire for fear of hitting friend as much as foe. Except for the sharp reports of musketry, the battle was now much like those of Salamis and Actium in the time of the Ancient Greeks and Romans. Ali Pasha had headed his damaged galley straight for Don John's flagship, holding his fire until the last moment. At almost point-blank range, his cannon fired first. The mainmast of the *Reale* was struck by a ricocheting ball; a whole bench of rowers was mown down, and bits of wood and human limbs were tossed into the air. The *Reale* was returning the fire as the two great galleys crashed into each other, splintering their long beaks.

The Spaniards twice boarded Ali's galley and twice were thrown back. Then the janissaries obtained a foothold on the *Reale* and began to gain

22

LEFT The scene aboard a Turkish galley during the battle.

ground. The splendid galley was in danger of falling to the enemy. But Colonna, the commander of the Papal forces, just then struck a decisive blow. He had boarded and stormed the ship that attacked him, and having thus disposed of his immediate adversary, saw the peril of the *Reale*. Manning all his oars, he drove the bow of his flagship deep into the stern of Ali's galley, swept her deck with a volley of musketry and sent a storming-party on to her poop. This timely aid was the turning point of the fight in the centre. Caught between two enemy forces, the janissaries were overwhelmed. Not one of the four hundred aboard the Turkish flagship survived, for no quarter was being given in this ferocious battle. Ali Pasha's head was cut off, placed on a pike, and carried to Don John with the captured standard of Mecca. The young admiral had the blood-dripping head thrown into the sea.

The battle had lasted nearly two hours so far. Along the left and centre the Christian galleys were storming or sinking those of the enemy which still maintained the fight. But the right wing, under Doria, had not yet engaged the enemy. These galleys were trailing away southward to the open sea, with

LEFT Galleys in action.

El Louck Ali and the Turkish left wing steering a parallel course. Some of Don John's captains who observed these movements thought that Doria was deserting or fleeing before El Louck Ali. Doria explained afterwards that he was trying to prevent an outflanking movement by the enemy. But it was the cunning Algerian who out-manœuvred the subtle Genoese. Having drawn Doria's galleys well away from the main battle, further than his own rearward vessels, El Louck Ali sent a signal down his line and turned suddenly to dash towards the fight in the centre.

The brunt of this onslaught fell upon the galleys of the Knights of Malta, on Don John's extreme right. One of the Order's galleys was captured and only three of its defenders survived, left for dead among the heaps of slain that encumbered the deck. Several more galleys were rushed and taken by El

BELOW The battle of Lepanto by C. J. Visscher, 1590.

Louck Ali's squadron, but that was the limit of his success. First Santa Cruz came hurrying to the rescue with the reserve; Don John, having overcome his immediate enemy, threw his galleys into the fray; and Doria, coming to his senses, thrust towards the thick of the battle. El Louck Ali saw that his attempt had failed, and thought only of escaping while there was time. Fighting his way clear, and helped by a following wind, he made off through the Straits of Ithaca with what remained of his squadron.

Santa Cruz and Doria pursued them for a while, but the fugitives had set their long lateen sails and gradually drew further away. A few other galleys had escaped back to Lepanto, but the great Turkish fleet had been largely destroyed. No less than 190 vessels were the prizes of the victors and 15 had been sunk. The estimate of Muslims killed or drowned was between twenty-five and thirty thousand, so terrible had been the slaughter. Ali Pasha's two sons and several of his best officers were among the few prisoners. But the success had been dearly bought. The Christian dead numbered about eight thousand, and the roll included many of the nobles and knights who had been in the forefront of the fighting. On the other hand, some ten thousand Christian galley-slaves were delivered from a living death at the rowing benches of the Muslims.

A gale sprang up as the October evening was deepening into darkness. Sails were hastily set; weary men pulled at the available oars; and Don John led his fleet to the shelter of a bay on the mainland. But first he sent off two fast galleys to carry news of the resounding victory to Messina; and from there the word went out to Rome and Venice, Naples, Genoa and Barcelona.

Lepanto was the last great battle between oar-driven navies. To all extents and purposes, the galleasses with their bristling batteries of guns represented the new type of warship that was soon to change the whole aspect of naval warfare.

3 'The most fortunate fleet'

The Spanish Armada, 1588

ABOVE The Duke of Medina Sedonia, the reluctant commander of the 'invincible armada'.

Seventeen years after Lepanto, Philip II of Spain undertook what he considered to be another crusade when he sent his Armada against England, hoping to invade and conquer that heretic country and bring it within the Roman Catholic faith again.

Spain had an excellent base in the Spanish Netherlands for assembling an invasion army, and the governor and commander of the Spanish forces there, the Duke of Parma, was an experienced general. But there remained the problem, as always, of getting an invasion army safely across the Straits of Dover. However, at that time the Spanish naval resources seemed strong enough – at least on paper – to be able to neutralize the English opposition

In late May 1588 the Spanish fleet began to work out of Lisbon river, led by the unwilling Duke of Medina Sidonia in his flagship *San Martin*, a 1,000-ton galleon mounting 48 guns. He had some 130 sail all told, carrying crews and soldiers totalling almost 30,000. There were the galleons of Portugal under the orders of Medina Sidonia himself and the galleons of Castile commanded by Diego Flores de Valdes – 20 powerful first-line ships, augmented by 4 galleasses of Naples. The second line was composed of 40 armed merchantmen; and there were 34 light, fast ships for scouting and dispatch-carrying, a squadron of unwieldy supply ships and 4 Portuguese galleys. Such was the *felicissima armada*, 'the most fortunate fleet', as it was called in official publications; though it was popularly called in Spain 'the invincible armada' as a tribute to its awesome strength.

Medina Sidonia's instructions from his king were simply to avoid action if possible and to concentrate on making rendezvous with the Duke of Parma 'off the cape of Margate', cover his landing and protect his line of supply. Three weeks after leaving Lisbon, when the armada had only just rounded Cape Finisterre, a great storm scattered the ships. Many days passed before the last of them struggled into Corunna or other northern Spanish ports. A month later, having repaired storm damage and taken fresh supplies on board, the armada sailed again for the English Channel, a brisk south wind filling its sails. The date was 12 July. (All the dates in this account are Old Style, that is, according to the Julian calendar, ten days behind the Gregorian proclaimed by Pope Gregory XIII in 1582. Most of the European countries were using the latter by 1588; but England was not – and did not accept it officially until 1752.)

On that very day in England, the Lord Admiral, Howard of Effingham, returned to Plymouth Sound with a fleet of ninety armed ships. He had gone to seek the Spaniards in their own waters, having received intelligence that they had regrouped at Corunna; but when halfway across the Bay of Biscay the north-east wind had hauled round to the south, and there was nothing for it but to turn and run back again.

A week later, on the afternoon of 19 July, the barque *Golden Hind* came bustling into Plymouth with news of the Spaniards. She was one of the

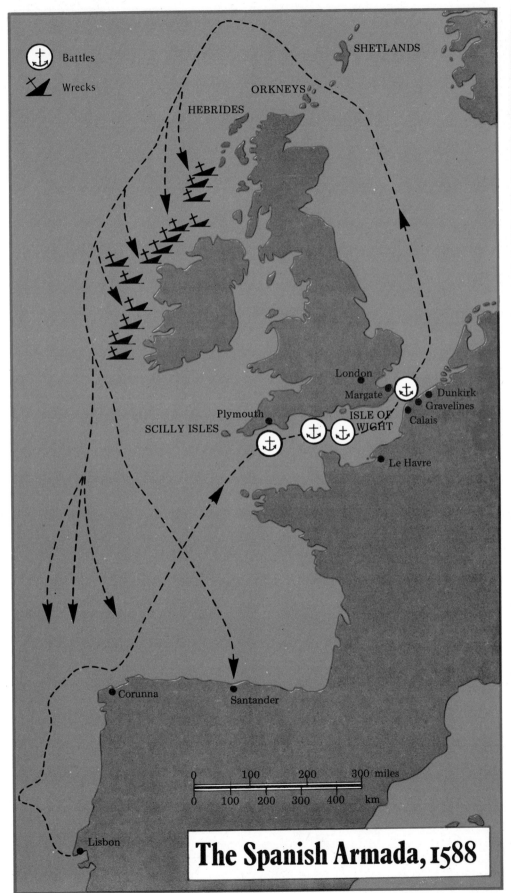

Battles

Wrecks

SHETLANDS

ORKNEYS

HEBRIDES

London
Margate
Plymouth
ISLE OF WIGHT
SCILLY ISLES
Dunkirk
Gravelines
Calais
Le Havre

Corunna
Santander

0   100   200   300 miles
0   100   200   300   400   km

Lisbon

The Spanish Armada, 1588

ABOVE Philip II of Spain.

RIGHT Elizabeth I of England.

screen assigned to cruise in the mouth of the Channel, and her captain, Thomas Fleming, reported sighting a large group of Spanish ships near the Scilly Isles. According to legend, Francis Drake was playing bowls on Plymouth Hoe when Fleming brought the news, and made his famous comment, 'There's time enough to finish the game.' In any case, the ships had to wait until the ebb tide that night, and then had to warp out of the Sound against a south-west breeze.

Two days later, the opposing fleets were in sight of one another. The Armada was moving up-Channel in a defensive, crescent formation, the strongest ships on the wings. As this great force was seen from the land, beacon after beacon roared into flame and the warning was carried from headland to headland, past Plymouth and all along the south coast to Dover, while other lines of beacons spread the news inland that the Spaniards had

LEFT Lord Admiral Charles Howard
of Effingham, Earl of Nottingham,
by Daniel Mytens. The background
battle represents his triumph
over the Armada.

BELOW Sir Francis Drake
by Nicholas Hilliard.

come at last. That night, the Armada still had the weather-gauge; but next
morning, 21 July, Howard 'recovered the wind of the Spaniards two leagues
to the westward of the Eddystone'. His ships had stood out to sea and then,
close hauled, had worked round the Armada's seaward wing and passed
astern. It was a fine feat of seamanship which surprised the Spaniards. The
English, for their part, were dismayed by the skilful and military precision of
the Spaniards' battle order. As they sized each other up, both sides must
have wondered how the battle would be fought. Never before had two such

large fleets met in combat; no one knew what were the best tactics or how effective ship artillery in great numbers could be.

The Spaniards continued to proceed up-Channel in stately formation, fending off the attacks of the English but not seeking action, as Medina Sidonia had ordered. Howard, for his part, wished to avoid a close fight at all costs, for the castles of the big Spanish ships loomed high above the English giving them great advantage if it came to grappling and boarding, and also with their musket-fire. So the English prudently kept their distance, subjecting the enemy ships to long-range bombardment. But none of the three clashes as the Armada moved up-Channel, closely pursued by the English, was in any way conclusive.

The first losses among the Armada were due to accident. One galleon, the 46-gun *Nuestra Señora del Rosario*, collided with another and lost her bowsprit and foremast; forsaken by the rest of the fleet, she was later snapped up by Drake in the *Revenge* as a prize. And an explosion aboard the *San Salvador* set her ablaze; the surviving crew were taken off and she was left to drift. Next day the waterlogged hulk was found by Captain Fleming, who had brought the first news of the Armada, and he towed the prize into Weymouth.

At dawn on 23 July the Armada had Portland Bill almost abeam, and the wind had hauled round to the northeast. Howard was to leeward, leading his line towards the land in an effort to work round the Spaniards' left wing and so recover the wind. It was a chance for Medina Sidonia to intercept and get to grips with the English ships, but they held off the Spanish by pouring in a series of broadsides. Both English and Spanish blazed away without doing each other much harm, but expended most of their powder and shot. By evening the wind was again fair from the west, which favoured the English strategically but enabled the Armada to plough steadily on again to its rendezvous with Parma.

Each side had learnt a lesson: the Spaniards that even when they had the weather-gauge they could not grapple and board the English ships, which were fast enough and weatherly enough to keep whatever distance they chose. The English had more big guns and of longer range, and better gunners who could fire much faster, though not accurately – but that was more the fault of the guns. The lesson for the English was that their shot inflicted no great harm and that although they were constantly reinforced from the south-coast ports and were able to bring the Spaniards to battle, they were quite unable to disrupt the Armada's orderly formation.

In an indecisive action off the Isle of Wight on 25 July the English tried to capture a couple of Spanish stragglers. There was hardly any wind, so three of the Neapolitan galleasses came rowing to their comrades' aid. Howard had earlier divided his force of about one hundred sail into four squadrons, and it was that commanded by John Hawkins which had managed to get within range of the two stragglers by ordering out boats to tow. For a while the two groups banged away at each other, with the rest of the fleets looking on. The Dons got the worst of the argument, and although their galleasses towed away the two stragglers, one of them was later swept on to the French coast near Le Havre and became a total wreck. This brought the Spanish losses in fighting ships to three only, and as the Armada drew ever nearer to the coast of Flanders Medina Sidonia had every reason to congratulate himself.

But the Spanish Commander-in-Chief was a worried man. He had had no word from Parma, although he had sent off several pinnaces with messages

LEFT A sixteenth-century map of Plymouth.

for him. The English were wearing down the Armada's strength with their long-range fire. Soon the Straits of Dover would be reached, and Medina Sidonia feared that once he passed through into the stormy, unfriendly North Sea he would be unable to rendezvous with Parma. So, as the Armada drew near Calais Roads late in the afternoon of 27 July, it struck its sails and its anchors thundered down. Medina Sidonia sent off more messengers to Parma's headquarters in Bruges and tried to obtain supplies of round and shot.

The English had dropped anchor too and were standing off 'just a long culverin-shot' (less than two miles) from the Spanish. Howard summoned Lord Seymour's squadron, which had been patrolling off the Flemish coast

BELOW An engraving by John Pine showing the capture of the galleon *Nuestra Señora del Rosario* by Drake in the *Revenge*.

RIGHT Two of John Pine's views of the Armada in the Channel.

for days past, and this reinforcement of 35 sail brought the strength of the English fleet to 140. But they were in an exposed anchorage and off an unfriendly shore. The Armada, it seemed, meant to ride here at anchor until Parma was ready and wind and weather served their purpose. The Dons had to be shifted, and soon. At Howard's council of war on the morning of the twenty-eighth there was general agreement. Nobody wanted to come to close quarters with the enemy ships or thought it would do much good to bombard them. There was only one way to shift them – with fireships.

Drake offered a ship of his own, and Hawkins one of his; amid mounting enthusiasm six more were recruited, and the captains scattered to the work of getting them ready. Their guns were left double-shotted, to go off when the

ABOVE John Hawkins.

blaze made them hot enough and to add to the destruction of the enemy.

Soon after midnight, when the set of the tide and a freshening wind aided the English endeavour, the Spaniards saw eight shapes belching flames and bearing down on them. A panic swept through their crowded anchorage. Most captains cut their cables and made for the open sea, scattering here and there in great confusion. The formidable Spanish order was broken at last. One great galleass, the *San Lorenzo*, fouled her rudder on a neighbour's cable and drifted ashore near the entrance to Calais harbour. At daybreak Howard ordered off some ships' boats to board and capture her. Meanwhile Drake had led the rest of the fleet to deal with the Spanish ships in sight. The English were bent on shortening the range, and their guns did real damage.

RIGHT The two fleets in combat off the Isle of Wight, from Saxton's Atlas.

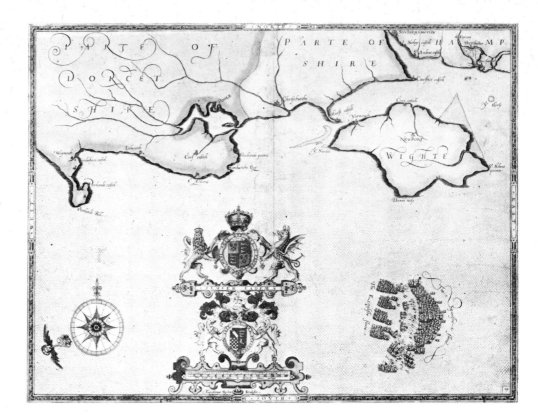

BELOW A contemporary map showing the Armada's route around England.

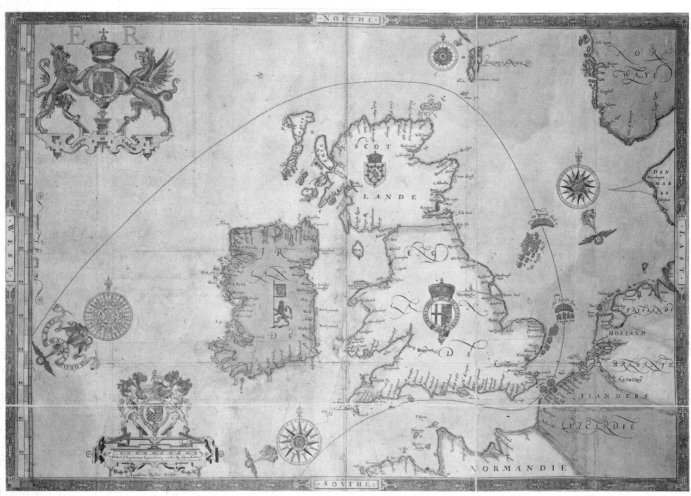

ABOVE The fire-ship attack on the Spanish fleet, 28 July 1588.

The battle took place off Gravelines, a little to the east of Dunkirk, and it lasted most of the day. There are conflicting reports as to the number of Spanish ships lost in that fateful action. But although it may not have been more than four or five, most of the other ships were certainly badly mauled and sustained heavy casualties. Moreover, towards the end of the afternoon the wind and the pressure of the English attack were driving the Spanish inexorably on to the Flanders shoals. Just when it seemed that in another hour most of the Armada would be aground – and the Spaniards were bracing themselves for the shock – there came a violent squall and the wind backed right round to the southwest. The battered Armada stood away northward, reformed into its tough, defensive crescent and sailed on into the North Sea.

There was no question now of a rendezvous with Parma and a landing on the English coast! Most of the ships were completely out of ammunition; fortunately for Medina Sidonia, the English were in no better case. Howard was without the means of bringing the Spaniards to action, and could only tag along behind. The wind held, and the two fleets sailed on northward, past the height of Hull, past the height of Berwick. On 2 August, in latitude 56° N, the English turned away. Howard was satisfied that the Spaniards did not intend to try for a landing, and all his ships were nearly out of food and water. Six days later they came scudding into Margate Roads and other havens round the Thames estuary, and dropped anchor. Howard had not lost a

37

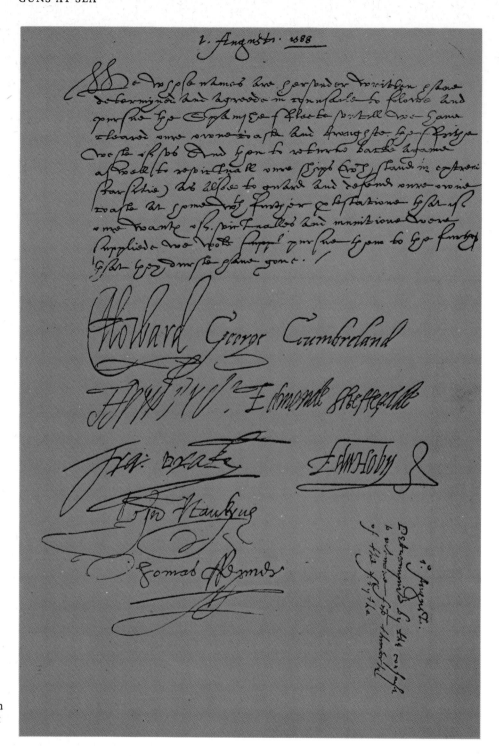

RIGHT The resolution of the English commanders' council of war to fight against the Spanish Armada.

single ship and casualties had not been serious. But the misfortunes of the Spaniards had only begun.

Although Medina Sidonia had lost only seven first-line ships, 'the invincible armada' was no longer a fighting force. A fifth of its men had been killed or disabled; morale of the others showed signs of cracking. Many ships were barely seaworthy; the *San Martin* leaked like a sieve, despite expert patching of the many shot-holes. The admiral and his council considered making for Norway but finally agreed to attempt the long road home round Scotland

and Ireland, in spite of the distance, the threat of starvation and the small amount of drinking water remaining. By 20 August they had cleared the Shetlands and were meeting the Atlantic billows. Now a much more deadly enemy than Howard and company was awaiting the crippled Armada.

All seemed to go well at first. The wind hauled round to the northeast, helping the ships on their homeward course. Medina Sidonia sent off a fast pinnace to report to King Philip and deliver to him the melancholy account of the campaign. But for the next two weeks the Armada met with nothing but storms from the worst possible quarter, the southwest, and with baffling head-winds. Nineteen ships were cast away on the rocks of the Hebrides or strewn along the unwelcoming shores of Ireland. It was not until the end of September that the last ships of the ill-fated enterprise straggled into the northern ports of Spain. The *San Martin* was one of them, with Medina Sidonia too weak to stand and 180 dead from scurvy or hunger and thirst.

In addition to the nineteen ships whose fate is known, thirty-five others were never heard of again. Only half of the Armada got back to Spain, but forty-four of them were galleons – two-thirds of the original fighting strength. They were all in evil case, and many were unfit for further service; but it was a considerable feat by Medina Sidonia to have got them home at all and said much for his powers of leadership.

4 America's First Naval Hero

Flamborough Head, 1779

His heroic actions had little influence upon the course of the American War of Independence, and he received no recognition until long after his death; but his tomb in the chapel of the Naval Academy at Annapolis is magnificent, and one of the first things that US naval cadets learn today is his defiant reply when called upon to surrender: 'I have not yet begun to fight!'

In 1777 the War was going badly for the British, and the French decided to intervene on the American side, seeing an opportunity of regaining some of their overseas possessions lost to Britain in past wars. The Americans had no navy, but from all along the east coast hardy seafarers poured forth as privateers to wage war against British trade. One such captain was John Paul Jones, who sailed from Virginia in November 1777 in command of an 18-gun sloop, the *Ranger*. He was a Scot, born near Kirkcudbright on the Solway Firth in 1747, had gone to sea at the age of twelve and by the time he was twenty had become skipper of a slaver out of Whitehaven, on the English side of Solway Firth; but in 1773 he had settled in Virginia.

The *Ranger* crossed the Atlantic and reached Nantes early in 1778 with two prizes taken on the way. She received from a French ship the first salute given to the thirteen-starred flag of the Union by a foreign ship. John Paul Jones put to sea again in April 1778, cruised up the Irish Sea and made several raids on the west coast of England. He landed at Whitehaven and set fire to its old fort, and in Solway Firth captured the frigate *Drake*, the first British warship to be taken by an American. On his return to France he was given command of a bigger ship, an old East Indiaman named *Duc de Duras*. Jones renamed her the *Poor Richard*, in honour of Benjamin Franklin's celebrated *Poor Richard's Almanack* (though the French insisted on calling the ship the *Bonhomme Richard*).

She was fitted out at Lorient and given a somewhat mixed armament – six 18-pounders on the lower gun-deck, twenty-eight 12-pounders on the upper gun-deck, and eight 9-pounders mounted fore and aft. The crew, too, were a mixed lot, with sailors of many nationalities. Captain Jones was also given a few small vessels for his 1779 campaign. When he sailed in August the *Poor Richard* was at the head of a division consisting of the *Alliance*, a 32-gun frigate commanded by a slightly-mad Frenchman named Landais, and two armed merchantmen, the 30-gun *Pallas* and the 12-gun *Vengeance*.

Jones took his little fleet through the Irish Sea and continued round the north of Scotland, capturing and destroying a few British vessels on the way. A raid into the Firth of Forth failed, due to adverse winds and a lack of co-operation from Landais, who had ideas of his own. Jones continued down the east coast of England and on 23 September, when off Flamborough Head, sighted a large convoy of British ships to seaward and on a south-westerly course. He signalled his small force to intercept.

It was a rich convoy from the Baltic, consisting of forty-one sail escorted by a powerful frigate, the 44-gun *Serapis*, Captain Richard Pearson, and an

auxiliary vessel, the 20-gun *Countess of Scarborough*. The encounter took place so close inshore that it was witnessed by a crowd of people on the cliffs between Flamborough and Scarborough; and they saw one of the fiercest combats in the history of sea warfare.

Captain Pearson's two ships had come between the convoy and its attackers, and the day was already well advanced when the fight began. The *Serapis* and the *Poor Richard* were running on a parallel course towards the shore, both on the port tack and within musket-range of each other; challenging cries and calls to surrender were passing from one ship to the other. The American opened fire first. The *Serapis* at once replied, and an explosion occurred in the *Poor Richard*. It was not, however, the British guns that had caused the damage; two of the 18-pounders had burst, and the lower gun-deck was already out of action.

The *Pallas* and the *Countess of Scarborough* engaged each other, but the *Alliance* contented herself with circling the combatants and firing on British and American alike, though with little effect. The *Poor Richard* was therefore left to fight a duel with an opponent which was a better sailer and had the

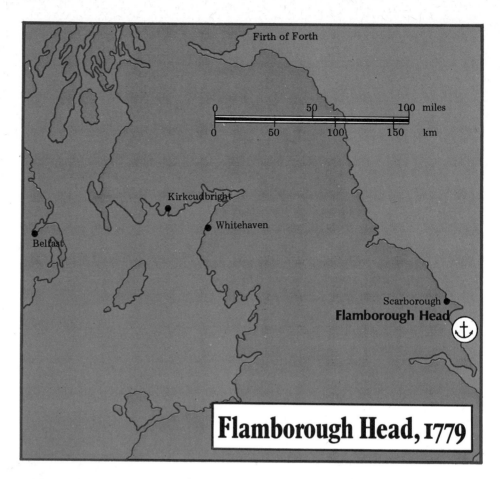

Firth of Forth

Kirkcudbright

Whitehaven

Belfast

Scarborough
Flamborough Head

Flamborough Head, 1779

BELOW A contemporary engraving of the *Serapis* and the *Poor Richard* grappling together. The American frigate *Alliance*, commanded by Pierre Landais, can be seen firing her guns on the right.

LEFT The capture of the *Serapis*.

heavier armament, and whose crew were decidedly better trained and disciplined than the motley crowd under Jones's orders. Before very long, the difference was making itself felt. The American ship was badly battered; many of her 12-pounders were put out of action, so that she was unable to fire a broadside, and only three of the 9-pounders were still serviceable. By then the crew were completely demoralized, and many of them wanted their captain to surrender.

'For the love of God, cap'n, strike!'

'No, I'll sink first!' he replied. 'Strike, never!' And, seizing his speaking-trumpet, he shouted across at Pearson, 'I have not yet begun to fight!'

RIGHT The battle of Flamborough
Head, from a nineteenth-century
French lithograph.

GUNS AT SEA

44

And, in fact, there was plenty to come. The *Poor Richard* was taking water in numerous places, and her captain realized that his only chance was to board and enter. The first attempt failed, but at the second Jones himself lashed the *Serapis*'s bowsprit to his own rigging, and the two ships swung together, bows to stern.

Pearson dropped anchor, hoping that the current would drag away the other ship; about forty of her crew were fighting their way along his deck, cutting down the English amid the tangle of fallen rigging. His gunners were firing into the hull of the *Poor Richard*, smashing it to pieces but killing no one, for all the crew were up above, at work with musket and cutlass. One of them tossed a grenade down a hatchway and it exploded in the powder-store, causing frightful damage to men and guns.

When the smoke cleared, the British were seen to be still defending themselves aft – and unexpected help seemed at hand. John Paul Jones had released his prisoners, the crews of the vessels he had captured and destroyed, as the *Poor Richard* seemed likely to sink at any moment. Their numbers could now swing the fight in Pearson's favour. Jones at once saw the peril, and with great resourcefulness and commanding presence ordered them to the pumps if they wanted to save their lives. They obeyed without a word.

It was at this point, when the battle had lasted three hours and the *Pallas* had captured the *Countess of Scarborough*, that Landais at last began to take an intelligent interest in events. He brought the *Alliance* round to port of the *Serapis*, his guns ready to rake that now defenceless ship. Pearson was obliged to strike his colours, just as his mainmast came crashing down.

The *Poor Richard* was sinking fast; Jones saved his victorious crew by transferring them to the defeated ship. A few days later he proudly brought the *Serapis*, flying the Union flag, to the Texel. But the Dutch refused to recognize the flag, so Jones sailed through the Channel in spite of the British and returned to Lorient.

Strange as it may seem, John Paul Jones was never given another command during the American War of Independence. Afterwards he served for a time in the Russian Navy with the rank of rear-admiral. He died in Paris, almost forgotten, in July 1792.

5 Far-reaching Consequences

Chesapeake Bay, 1781

It was not in European waters, however, that the American War of Independence was being decided, but across the Atlantic. The chief question was whether Britain could maintain command of the Atlantic approaches, to keep open her supply lines. Only the French were capable of disputing it; and for once they had the stronger fleet and no war to sustain in Europe.

French squadrons convoyed troops to help Washington and also locked up the British garrisons in the West Indies; Dominica, St Vincent and Grenada fell, and then the harbourage of Newport, which obliged the British to withdraw their troops from Rhode Island to reinforce New York. In July 1780 a French expeditionary force under General Rochambeau was able to land at Newport without opposition. And it was Rochambeau, supported by a squadron under Admiral François de Grasse, who did much to bring about an American victory in the autumn of 1781.

De Grasse sailed from Brest for the West Indies in March 1781 with a fleet of twenty line-of-battle ships, a proportionate number of frigates and many transports and supply ships. De Grasse was sixty years of age and had seen much active service since leaving the naval school at Toulon in his late teens. He arrived at Martinique with his ships at the end of April. Avoiding a British squadron commanded by Rear-Admiral Sir Samuel Hood, he captured St Lucia, then made for San Domingo (the French-held part of Haiti)

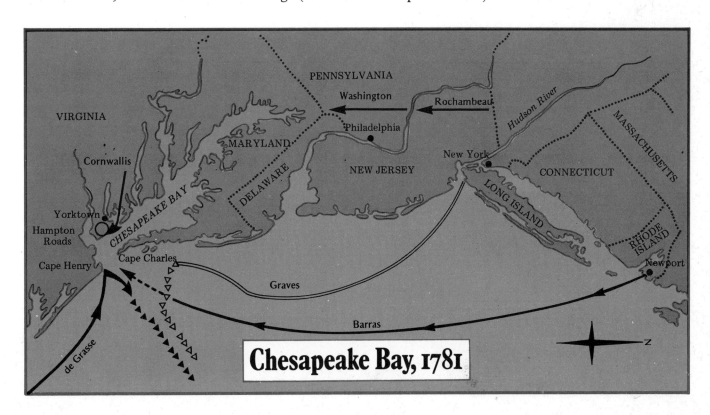

Chesapeake Bay, 1781

ABOVE Admiral François de Grasse, a coloured lithograph from a portrait by A. Maurin.

BELOW The English fleet attacking the French at the mouth of the Chesapeake.

to embark the garrison, these troops being intended as reinforcements for General Rochambeau. While there, the frigate *Concorde* arrived with despatches for him from Rochambeau. De Grasse learnt that a small squadron commanded by Barras de St Laurent had arrived at Newport with more reinforcements for Rochambeau, and that the latter – having consulted Washington – left it to De Grasse to decide the best way in which the naval forces could support the land operations. The British, Rochambeau reported, were then advancing through Carolina and Virginia towards Chesapeake Bay, while Rochambeau was crossing Connecticut to join up with Washington.

The alternative before De Grasse was whether to make for the region of New York, which was the chief British base, or for Hampton Roads (the mouth of the Chesapeake) where he would be able to give closer support to the Franco-American armies. He decided in favour of the latter and sent the *Concorde* back to Newport to inform Rochambeau, while he set sail, keeping to leeward of the Bahamas and then stealing up the coast of the mainland.

Hood, meanwhile, had been searching for the French squadron since missing it off St Lucia, and had sent off a corvette, the *Swallow*, to inform Rear-Admiral Thomas Graves, who was in command of a strong force then moored in the mouth of the Hudson. But the *Swallow* was intercepted by four American privateers, and Graves never received the despatches.

Hood took the shortest route across to the Chesapeake, while the French were creeping up the coast, and arrived in Hampton Roads on 25 August to

A View of the English Fleet of 19 Sail of the Line under Rear Admiral Graves Attacking the French Fleet of 24 Sail of the Line under Count De Grasse coming out of the Chesapeak the 5th September 1781.

find the anchorage empty. Having satisfied himself that no enemy ships were in the neighbourhood, he continued northward and three days later cast anchor at the entrance to the Hudson, well satisfied at having got ahead of De Grasse and barred the way to him.

However, five days after Hood had sailed from Hampton Roads, De Grasse arrived there and anchored inside Cape Henry. He put his troops ashore, conferred with Washington, and then sent two pairs of ships to blockade the rivers James and York. The British troops under Cornwallis were thus invested by land and sea, and shut themselves up in Yorktown.

Now that Hood had joined him, Graves was in command of more than twenty warships. They sailed south with the object of helping Cornwallis. Hood had the van and was flying his flag in the 100-gun *Barfleur*, Graves commanded the main body in his 108-gun *London*, and the rear was under the command of Samuel Francis Drake in the 82-gun *Princessa*. In this formation, with the wind almost dead astern, they were approaching the entrance to the Chesapeake when the presence of a few suspicious sail was signalled. Graves, believing he had to deal with a small division at most, crowded on sail. . . .

It was ten in the morning of 5 September 1781. The French, too, were so little expecting to see a strong enemy squadron that many of their ships' crews were ashore or ferrying boats across the bay with supplies for the army. When some sails were sighted, they were at first thought to belong to Barras's division, which was expected with troop reinforcements from Newport. But then the guard frigates came scudding back, firing their guns to announce the strength of the enemy – ten, twenty-five, ultimately twenty-seven vessels of which nineteen were men-of-war. The British, obviously. There was no time to spare. However, the wind was coming off the sea, the tide was still mounting, so that in order to stand out to sea the French ships had to beat about interminably in the three-mile-wide channel. To gain time, De Grasse ordered the ships to slip their cables; in those days, weighing the anchor was a long, man-handling process.

BELOW A view of the action off the Chesapeake by Theodore Gudin.

49

RIGHT Rear-Admiral Thomas
Graves, a mezzotint after a portrait
by James Northcote.

Admiral Graves missed a golden opportunity. If, as Hood suggested, he
had attacked each ship as she came tacking slowly out of the bay – and the
British had the wind in their favour – he could have destroyed the French van
before the rest of the squadron was out. Instead, he gave the French all the
time they needed, until they were formed in line abreast, though in the order
in which the ships had cleared the bay, not in their theoretical stations in the
line, and with the van well ahead. Graves, meanwhile, was deploying to port,
so that the squadrons should face each other in two long lines. His intention
was to engage the enemy in the dignified, orderly manner of van against van,
centre against centre, rear against rear. He still had the weather-gauge, and
therefore the initiative, but unfortunately the sacrosanct 'Fighting Instructions' of the Admiralty contained no signal corresponding exactly to the
situation; and the signals he made to remedy matters somewhat baffled his
captains. It was unfortunate, too, that the movement had brought Drake's
division into the van – 'an officer with a great name but of moderate worth,'
as an American historian recently wrote – and left Hood's in the rear, where
he was unable to influence the main action.

When Graves signalled 'Prepare to attack', the commander of the French van, Bougainville, veered away instead of continuing to tack into the wind; this had the effect of delaying the beginning of the action and enabling De Grasse and the rest of the squadron to get into proper station. Moreover, Hood had continued in line ahead, maintaining that the signal was still hoisted in the *London*, instead of bearing down on the French centre.

In short, it was four in the afternoon before action was joined, the fifth ship in the French line, the *Réfléchi*, being hit first and her captain killed. The first few minutes were the worst, in fact, for the four or five leading French ships, which came under fire from seven or eight of the enemy van. Drake's flagship set the *Diadème* on fire and he was about to board her when the *St Esprit* came to her aid, opening fire with such terrible effect that the *Princessa* backed and drew away. Bougainville, in the *Auguste*, was engaged in a duel with the *Terrible*, which got so much the worst of it that she had to be abandoned four days later.

ABOVE Louis-Antoine de Bougainville, the commander of the French van.

After this opening clash, the French soon gained the ascendancy, and Graves eventually drew off. The French were still to leeward and so unable to continue the action. For five days the two squadrons remained within sight of each other. Then came a sudden shift of wind, and De Grasse, convinced by now that Barras had safely reached the Chesapeake, returned to his anchorage.

The French casualties amounted to 220, the British to 336, but the damage to British vessels was greatly disproportionate to the French. The *Princessa* had lost her main-topmast, the *Shrewsbury* her main and fore-topmast, the *Intrepid* had her topsail-yard splintered and her lower masts were in a bad state; the *Ajax* was holed and taking almost as much water as the *Terrible*, while the *Montagu*'s rigging looked likely to collapse at any moment. But only two of the French ships, the *Diadème* and the *Caton*, had suffered any serious damage.

The real outcome of the battle, however, was that the whole strategic situation of the war had definitely swung in favour of the French and the Americans. Barras had indeed reached the Chesapeake with reinforcements. De Grasse now had thirty-six warships under his command and could confidently withstand any further sea offensive; but none came. Freed of threats from the sea, Washington and Rochambeau tightened their grip on Yorktown, and Cornwallis capitulated on 19 October. The American War of Independence was practically lost for the British, chiefly due to De Grasse having gained command of the sea at the right moment. As the American historian S. E. Morison recently wrote: 'Without De Grasse's victory off the Virginia Capes, it is not Cornwallis's capitulation but Washington's that history would have recorded at Yorktown.'

The following year, Admiral Lord Rodney defeated De Grasse at the battle of the Saints, off Guadeloupe. Technical improvements in British gunnery and Rodney's dashing tactics were too much for the French. Five of their ships were captured, including the flagship, and De Grasse was taken prisoner to England. However, this British victory came too late to affect the result of the war. The Americans had obviously won, and a separate peace settlement was signed with them in November 1782.

6 Mutinous but Victorious

Cape St Vincent, 1797

The notorious mutinies in the British fleet at the end of the eighteenth century were based on very real grievances. The country had been engaged in almost continuous war at sea for the past one hundred years, yet during that long period there had been no improvement in conditions for the lower deck. Pay had not been increased since the reign of Charles II, and even this pittance was withheld until a ship was paid off, leaving wives and children to starve meantime. A sailor wounded in action had no claim to any pay while unable to serve. Rations were bad and fraudulently administered. The chief demands of the men were eventually met, but not before blood had been shed and the safety of the country placed in jeopardy.

It is remarkable that during this period when the morale of the Navy was very low, Britain won two famous victories at sea. Admiral Adam Duncan crushed a Dutch squadron at Camperdown, and Admiral Sir John Jervis inflicted much damage upon a superior Spanish force off Cape St Vincent.

Jervis was cruising off the west coast of Spain with fifteen ships-of-the-line when, at dawn on 14 February 1797, a Spanish squadron was sighted making for Cadiz. The British were sailing in two divisions, one of seven ships, the other of eight; the Spanish force was in loose formation, and the half a dozen ships in the van were far ahead of the rest.

'A victory is very essential to England at this moment,' Jervis murmured to his flag-captain when the Spanish were first sighted. Their numbers went on increasing until twenty-seven were counted. 'Never mind,' he said. 'Even if there are fifty sail I will go through them!'

'Very good, Sir John,' said the captain. 'We'll give them a damned good licking!'

This was the spirit in which Jervis decided to cut through the huge gap in the Spanish formation. However, some six tense hours passed before the British were in firing range. In those days there was plenty of time to prepare for the slaughter. The gun-decks were cleared of everything but fighting-equipment, and they were sanded to prevent the gun-crews slipping in the blood that would flow around their feet. Huge nets were spread above the bulwarks to keep off enemy boarders; down below the waterline, the surgeons laid out their grisly instruments.

The Spanish also had time to reduce the gap in their line. Commodore Horatio Nelson, flying his broad pendant in the third-rate 74-gun *Captain*, saw that the enemy could unite in a single line before action could be joined. Although he was last but two in his column, he at once wore the *Captain* out of the line, put the helm hard over and sped into the fast-closing gap, engaging half a dozen Spanish ships single-handed. Three of them had more than one hundred guns, and one, the *Santissima Trinidad*, was the only four-decker ever launched and probably the largest ship in the world at that time.

It was perhaps the most remarkable act of courage in Nelson's career – to leave the order of battle without instructions from the commander-in-chief.

RIGHT Nelson boarding the *San Nicolas* from his ship the *Captain*, after a painting by Frank Baden-Powell.

Such an act usually resulted in a court-martial, disgrace and ruin. But Jervis recognized the need and at once ordered two ships to go to Nelson's assistance. They were the *Culloden* and the *Excellent*, commanded by his old friends Troubridge and Collingwood. The latter was the first to join him; so well-trained were the *Excellent*'s gunners that they could deliver ten broadsides for each one fired by a Spanish ship, and their intensity soon compelled two of the enemy to lower their colours.

54

Nelson's action had not been as suicidal as it looked. After the first broadside, targets were obscured by smoke and the massed Spanish ships were often firing into each other; most of them were under-manned and the crews raw. Nevertheless the *Captain* was disabled before support reached her; she lost her fore-topmast, and the wheel and much of the rigging were shot away. Nelson decided to board the nearest enemy ship, the 80-gun *San Nicolas*, and to board her himself, an unprecedented action for a

LEFT Nelson boarding the *San Josef*, after a painting by H. Singleton.

ABOVE Nelson painted by Heinrich Schmidt in 1800.

LEFT The battle of Cape St Vincent by Richard Paton.

commodore. As the two ships ground together, British seamen and marines armed with cutlasses and pistols sprang for the enemy deck. A marine smashed a cabin window and jumped in, followed by Nelson. Soon the *San Nicolas* was taken and her colours hauled down. A first-rate, the 112-gun *San Josef*, lying alongside her began firing on the British boarders. Nelson and his men instantly passed over to this ship, swarming on to her deck with such impetus that the Spanish captain at once surrendered. 'And so', wrote Nelson in his memorandum after the battle, 'on the quarter-deck of a Spanish First-rate, extravagant as the story may seem, did I receive the Swords of the vanquished Spaniards, which as I received I gave to William Fearney, one of my bargemen, who placed them, with the greatest sang-froid, under his arm.'

Meanwhile Jervis with the bulk of his squadron had been trying to bring about a *mêlée* with the main Spanish force; but the latter's chief anxiety was to get away, not to extend the action, and they made all sail to the southward. Even so, the victory was decisive. The *Santissima Trinidad*, the Spanish flagship, had been dismasted and Admiral Cordoba had found it necessary to shift his flag to a frigate. Four prizes had been taken, two of them by Nelson. This was considerable for a squadron little more than half the size of the enemy. Moreover they had been taken with a modest toll of life, seventy-three in all. Of these, the *Captain* had twenty-four killed, the *Excellent* eleven, the *Culloden* ten, and the *Blenheim* – the third ship to go to Nelson's assistance – twelve. As Jervis said: 'The ships' returns of killed and wounded, although not always the criterion of their being more or less in action, is in this instance correctly so.'

But the tangible result of this victory was as nothing compared with its psychological effect: British morale at home shot up.

7 The Nelson Touch

Trafalgar, 1805

Napoleon never understood that naval squadrons could not be moved about like army corps. His plans for the invasion of England were beset by the same problem as had faced King Philip of Spain – how to obtain a passage across the Channel for his troops encamped at Boulogne. The French squadrons at Brest and Rochefort were being blockaded by the British under Cornwallis and Stirling, and the Toulon squadron was being watched by Nelson. So Napoleon devised a large-scale diversion to draw off the British squadrons and enable Vice-Admiral Ganteaume to come out of Brest and head up-Channel to the Straits. The main effort would be made by the Toulon squadron commanded by Vice-Admiral Pierre Villeneuve, recently appointed to the Mediterranean command at the age of forty-one. He was to embark troops and sail for the West Indies, capture some British possessions and strengthen the garrison on Haiti, then return to Europe.

Villeneuve duly sailed on 30 March 1805 with twenty ships and some transports. On 9 April he was joined off Cadiz by a few Spanish warships under Admiral Gravina, for Spain had again declared war against England at the end of 1804 – reluctantly and under pressure from Napoleon. Nelson's squadron was off the southern end of Sardinia when, on 4 April, a scouting frigate brought news of having seen Villeneuve's squadron at sea, sixty miles south-west of Toulon, on 31 March. Nelson thought that Villeneuve's destination was Egypt, and he took up position between Sardinia and Tunisia to bar the way. It was only on 16 April that he heard Villeneuve had stood away from Cadiz and sailed for the West Indies. Despite the long start of the French, he decided to go in pursuit, but adverse winds kept him in the Mediterranean for another three weeks. Nevertheless he was at Barbados on 4 June, just in time to deter Villeneuve from attacking the island. The French admiral learnt of his arrival and promptly sailed for Europe. Nelson was only four days behind him now, but without knowledge of the course he was taking.

On 17 July Nelson and his squadron were in sight of Cape St Vincent, and went on to Gibraltar to take in fresh supplies. Nothing had been seen of the French, and Nelson discovered the reason a few days later when a brig arrived from England and he received the latest gazettes. An item caught his eye: the *Curious* had arrived at Plymouth on 7 July. She was the brig that Nelson had speeded home from the West Indies in advance of his squadron to give the Admiralty the latest information about his movements. The gazette also announced that a week after the brig's departure she had sighted the French in the Atlantic, standing to the northward about three hundred miles to the north of Antigua. This made the situation clearer to Nelson. Villeneuve had not, then, made for Cadiz but had sailed on a course farther to the north and was heading for some port in the Bay of Biscay. Nelson had been looking for him too much to the south; so, without wasting a moment, he took advantage of a fresh easterly wind and headed into the Atlantic.

ABOVE Napoleon by Robert Lefevre.

BELOW Vice-Admiral Pierre Villeneuve, commander-in-chief of the French fleet at Trafalgar.

RIGHT Lord Nelson by
Francis Abbot.

Again his quarry eluded him – though Villeneuve knew no more of
Nelson's movements than the latter knew of his. On 22 July Villeneuve was
120 miles off Cape Finisterre when he sighted a squadron of fifteen ships
commanded by Sir Robert Calder; they were some of the dispositions made
by Barham, the First Sea Lord, on receipt of the news brought by the
Curious. The action which ensued was an indeterminate affair, fought in a
thick mist. Villeneuve broke away after losing two of the Spanish ships and
made for the shelter of Spanish coastal waters. Then, as he had many sick
men and most of his ships were short of food and water, he took the squadron
to Cadiz, where he arrived on 19 August.

Nelson had missed his opportunity by just two or three days. He had
passed westward of Villeneuve through heading out into the Atlantic; then
he had pressed on to reach what he considered the danger spot – Cornwallis's
station at the western approaches to the Channel. Leaving most of his ships

LEFT Admiral Lord Collingwood by Henry Howard.

with Cornwallis, he proceeded in his ship the *Victory* to Portsmouth.

Cornwallis had earlier moved some one hundred miles south-west from Brest, in compliance with orders sent out by Barham by a fast frigate. But he was back on station a week later; and despite Napoleon's urgent demands, Ganteaume had failed to take the Brest squadron to sea while the blockade was raised.

OPPOSITE TOP A contemporary cartoon commenting on the discrepancies in the distribution of prize money – a captain at Trafalgar received £973 while a sailor was given £1 17s 6d.

OPPOSITE BOTTOM Nelson's final entry in his diary, Monday, 25 October 1805.

While Napoleon was sending courier after courier to Villeneuve, exhorting him to sail for the Channel, Nelson was returning to Spanish waters in the *Victory*, having had news of Villeneuve's presence at Cadiz. By the end of September Nelson was again in control of the Mediterranean squadron. He stood away from Cadiz with most of the ships, well out of sight, some fifty miles to the westward, leaving a few frigates to keep close watch on Cadiz.

There were twenty-seven ships-of-the-line waiting for Villeneuve to come out, hoping that he would come out. In fact he had received fresh orders from Napoleon, who had started the Austrian campaign: he was to break out and return to the Mediterranean. Meanwhile Nelson did everything possible to ensure that the battle would be a British victory. He had his captains to dine with him aboard the *Victory* and expounded his plans, which were the subject of a tactical memorandum that he issued on 9 October. The business of getting into a long line of battle was considered outdated. In future, the order of sailing was to be the order of battle, and this would be in two columns heading for the enemy line to break it up and cause a general *mêlée*. This was 'the Nelson touch'. The enemy would be presented with the highly desired opportunity to 'cross the T', and doubly so, with the British advancing in two columns in line ahead; and there would be some unpleasant minutes for the leading ships, when the enemy guns would be able to rake them before they could bring their own fire to bear. But it was a risk worth taking. French gunners still aimed at masts and rigging in the hope of disabling an adversary and forcing her to fall out of the line, whereas the British believed in making the hull their target, aiming 'between wind and water' to start dangerous leaks.

The tactics to be employed were thoroughly gone over, so there would be little need of signals. Besides, Nelson's memorandum contained that magnificent phrase, 'but in case signals cannot be seen, or clearly understood, no captain can do very wrong if he places his ship alongside that of an enemy'.

The hoped-for signal, 'the enemy ships are coming out of port', was made on the morning of 19 October by the frigate *Sirius*, the nearest to Cadiz, and

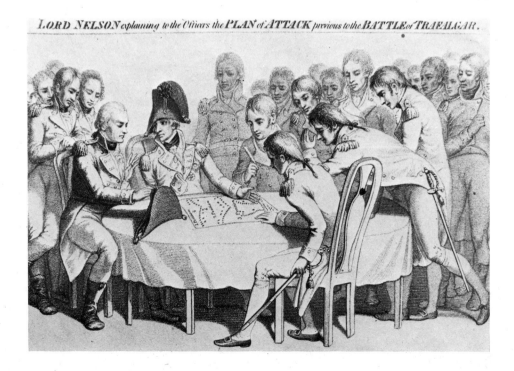

LORD NELSON explaining to the Officers the PLAN of ATTACK previous to the BATTLE of TRAFALGAR.

RIGHT A popular print of Nelson explaining the plan of attack at Trafalgar to his officers.

EQUITY or a Sailors PRAYER before BATTLE. *Anecdote of the Battle of Trafalgar.*

ABOVE Nelson on the quarter-deck of the *Victory* before Trafalgar.

relayed to the *Victory*, fifty miles to the westward. Nelson's ships made sail and stood away in the two columns in which they would give battle. But another two days were to pass before then.

Villeneuve had thirty-three ships, of which fifteen were Spanish under the command of Admiral Gravina, who heartily detested the French. He had fought against them twelve years previously, at Toulon, alongside Admiral Hood. His was an independent command, though his instructions were to give the French every assistance. Villeneuve had to use the utmost tact to obtain his agreement on the order of battle – which was far from respected, anyway.

About six in the evening of 20 October Villeneuve's frigates signalled that the enemy had been sighted to windward. Throughout the night the combined fleet continued standing to the southward, with the British about fifteen miles to windward. Soon after daybreak on the twenty-first the opposing forces were in clear view of each other, with the British steering in two groups for the centre and rear of the French and Spanish. Villeneuve made a signal to form a single line of battle, on the starboard tack. Confusion resulted. The swell was increasing, but the westerly wind was still light. Not until eleven o'clock, with the enemy drawing near, was the combined fleet in anything approaching orderly disposition. It stretched from north to south, and was some twenty-seven miles south-south-west of Cadiz.

Nelson had hoisted the signal to form order of sailing in two columns. Now that he had the enemy in sight at last, he could not get at him quick enough; the pace was stately, the wind still slight. Collingwood, in the *Royal Sovereign*, was in no less of a hurry. 'Make more sail,' he signalled to his line. And Nelson, goaded by this, ordered such a press of sail as none of the crew could remember having seen on a ship going into action. The two old friends seemed to have no other thought than to race to be the first to engage the enemy. Each was at the head of his column.

By hoisting the studding-sails, the *Royal Sovereign* gained a little extra speed – and the privilege of being the first to open fire on the enemy, and to be for some minutes without close support! Raked by shot from the Spanish 112-gun *Santa Anna* and her neighbouring ships, the *Royal Sovereign* continued straight on course; sixty men were killed or wounded, but then she broke the enemy line just astern of the *Santa Anna* and poured in broadside after broadside, inflicting 250 casualties in the Spanish ship.

The *Victory* had a similar opening duel as she pierced the line between Villeneuve's flagship, the *Bucentaure*, and the *Redoutable*. The general

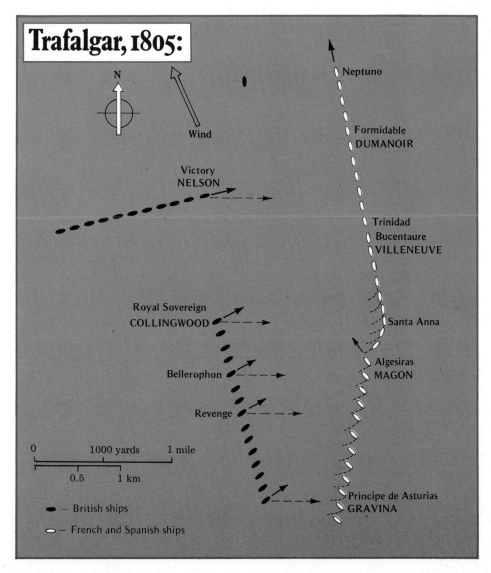

Trafalgar, 1805:

N

Wind

Victory
NELSON

Neptuno

Formidable
DUMANOIR

Trinidad
Bucentaure
VILLENEUVE

Royal Sovereign
COLLINGWOOD

Santa Anna

Bellerophon

Algesiras
MAGON

Revenge

Principe de Asturias
GRAVINA

0   1000 yards   1 mile

0.5   1 km

– British ships

– French and Spanish ships

OVERLEAF The *Redoutable* at Trafalgar by A. E. Mayer.

mêlée that ensued gave great advantage to the British. Nevertheless they were in a risky situation, due to their plunge into the enemy line; this, being in the form of a crescent, gave the van an opportunity to tack and bear down to encircle the *Victory* and the leading ships before those in the rear could arrive within range, because of the slight wind. But the French rear-admiral, Dumanoir, proved incapable of such initiative.

The *Redoutable* tried to fill the gap in the French line, and in order to avoid a collision Nelson gave the order to port the helm earlier than he had intended. The *Victory* not only lost way, but her mizzen- and fore-topmasts went, falling on to the *Redoutable* as the two ships ranged close alongside. They were soon locked in death-grips, muzzles nearly touching. The firing from the *Redoutable*'s fighting-tops almost cleared the decks of the *Victory*, and there was some danger that she would be boarded. But then the *Temeraire* ranged up on the starboard side and poured such a fire into the *Redoutable* that two hundred of her crew were killed or wounded.

The battered *Victory* was able to draw off, but Nelson had received his death wound. His uniform and decorations had attracted the fire of a sharp-shooter from a fighting-top in the *Redoutable*; the ball had penetrated Nelson's chest and lodged in his spine. He was carried down to the cockpit and died about three hours later.

The battle had continued under the direction of Collingwood, though in truth no direction was needed, for Nelson had made all necessary signals. It was reported that Collingwood had shown some impatience, just before the action began, on seeing various flags being hoisted in the *Victory*. 'What is Nelson signalling about? We all know what we have to do.' It was the now celebrated signal, 'England expects that every man will do his duty'.

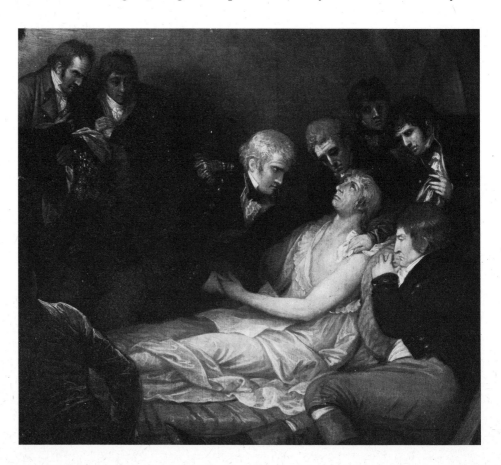

RIGHT The death of Nelson by Benjamin West.

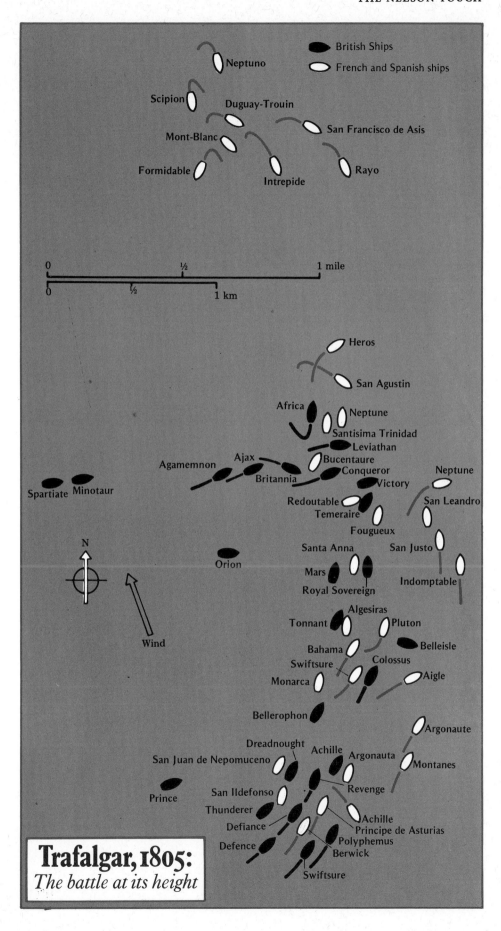

British Ships
French and Spanish ships

Neptuno

Scipion

Duguay-Trouin

San Francisco de Asis

Mont-Blanc

Formidable

Intrepide

Rayo

0 ½ 1 mile
0 ½ 1 km

Heros

San Agustin

Africa

Neptune

Santisima Trinidad

Leviathan

Bucentaure

Agamemnon   Ajax

Conqueror

Neptune

Britannia

Victory

Spartiate Minotaur

Redoutable

San Leandro

Temeraire

Fougueux

San Justo

N

Santa Anna

San Justo

Orion

Mars

Indomptable

Royal Sovereign

Algesiras

Wind

Tonnant

Pluton

Belleisle

Bahama

Colossus

Swiftsure

Aigle

Monarca

Bellerophon

Argonaute

Dreadnought

Achille

Argonauta

Montanes

San Juan de Nepomuceno

Revenge

Prince

San Ildefonso

Achille

Thunderer

Principe de Asturias

Defiance

Polyphemus

Defence

Berwick

Swiftsure

Trafalgar, 1805:
The battle at its height

ABOVE The battle of Trafalgar
by J. W. M. Turner.

RIGHT The deployment of the
opposing fleets at Trafalgar.

The *Santa Anna*, completely dismasted by the guns of the *Royal Sovereign*, struck her colours at a quarter-past-two. She had, however, done much damage to Collingwood's ship, which had lost her main- and mizzen-masts. A little later, the *Fougueux* surrendered; she had gone to the assistance of the Spanish ship, been attacked by the *Royal Sovereign*, the *Mars* and the *Tonnant* (a former French ship, captured at the Battle of the Nile), and was finally boarded by the *Temeraire*. The *Monarca*, too, had struck. In the *Algesiras*, Rear-Admiral Magon was killed, his flag-captain wounded, as were the two officers who successively took over command; dismasted and on fire, her colours were hauled down. The captain of the *Aigle* was killed too, and his first lieutenant badly wounded; with all her masts gone and her rigging swept away, after a terrific duel with the *Defiance*, she struck her colours at half-past-three. By then, three more French ships had surrendered: the *Swiftsure*, with nearly four feet of water in her hold and three masts gone by the board; the *Berwick* (like the *Swiftsure*, a British ship captured several years before), which had lost her two senior officers; and the *Redoutable*, which was so entangled with the *Temeraire* that the latter did not manage to free herself until seven in the evening.

The *Bucentaure* and the *Santissima Trinidad*, the two ships which had borne the full fury of the enemy attack, fought side by side until completely dismasted. The French flagship was in danger of sinking, and Villeneuve wished to shift his flag to another ship and endeavour to save what remained of the combined fleet. But none of the *Bucentaure*'s boats was seaworthy. The *Santissima Trinidad* was hailed, but she was about to surrender. Villeneuve abandoned the fight, and the *Bucentaure* was secured by the *Conqueror*.

ABOVE The battle of Trafalgar by W. E. D. Stuart.

OVERLEAF The *Victory* is towed towards Gibraltar after the battle of Trafalgar.

71

Five more Spanish ships surrendered, and the *Neptuno*, one of the van, was captured at a quarter-past-five, by which time the battle had practically ended. There were dismasted and disabled ships of both sides scattered over a wide area of sea. But not a single British ship had struck, and seven French and twelve Spanish ships were in their enemy's possession. The remainder of the combined fleet, some seven or eight ships, were retreating towards Cadiz led by the *Principe de Asturias*, in which Admiral Gravina had been mortally wounded. Dumanoir drew off to the west with four of his ships; although they had taken little part in the fighting, it had been enough for them to be in need of some repair.

Collingwood was left with his prizes and with another enemy to face – the gale, which the swell had been heralding since early morning. Few of the British ships were capable of bearing sail. They rode out the storm with much difficulty, the south-westerly threatening to drive them on to the sharp reefs of Cape Trafalgar a few miles to leeward. Fortunately the howling wind shifted a little to the north, else all the prizes and the dismasted British ships would inevitably have foundered. The prisoners under hatches were released to help the depleted crews in their struggles against the elements. The battered *Redoutable* – which was being towed by the *Swiftsure* – went down with 156 men on board; and the *Fougueux* was driven ashore and wrecked, though 120 men were saved from her. The *Conqueror* was obliged to cast off the *Bucentaure*, and the French ship was driven on to the reefs and began to break up; five hundred men were rescued from her by the *Indomptable*, then she in turn foundered, and all except 150 of those on board were lost.

Collingwood realized that it was impossible to retain the remaining captured ships, and sank or burnt the worst damaged among them. Only four were brought safely into Gibraltar: the French *Swiftsure* and the Spanish *Bahama*, *San Ildefonso* and *San Juan Nepomuceno*. Four other prizes were brought into Plymouth several weeks later. These were the four ships of Dumanoir's division; they were caught off Finisterre on 4 November by Commodore Strachan, who was in command of four ships-of-the-line and four frigates, and were captured after Dumanoir had put up as decided a fight as his showing at Trafalgar had been timid.

So ended Napoleon's grand plan and Villeneuve's attempt, begun a year previously when he had taken over the Toulon command. The unhappy man did not long survive his victor at Trafalgar. Villeneuve was a prisoner in England for four months, and was then freed and returned to France. A few days later, on 21 April 1806, he was found dead in an hotel at Rennes. Whether he committed suicide or was the victim of a political assassination is not known; the mysterious circumstances of his death have never been satisfactorily explained.

8 The last Battle fought under Sail

Navarino, 1827

Twenty-two years after Trafalgar, British and French sailors fought on the same side, together with Russians. This was at the Battle of Navarino, where in the cause of Greek independence the Allied force was aligned against Turks and Egyptians. The already complicated situation was made more so when a Greek naval division commanded by a British officer also put in an appearance. Indeed, this multi-national battle was fought in extraordinary confusion. What is more, not one of the nations involved was officially at war with another. Nor is it known who fired the first shot.

The political situation which led to the confrontation taking place was almost as confusing. In 1821 the Greeks had risen against their Turkish overlords, and enthusiasm for their cause spread throughout Europe; ships and money and volunteers were raised for the rebels, especially in England. However, British and French commercial interests were involved, and Russia saw an opportunity to gain control of the Dardanelles and obtain access to the Mediterranean. The British Foreign Minister, Canning, tried to mediate and prevent any great Power using force. That hope vanished when the Turks called to their aid the army and fleet of their ally Mehemet Ali, Pasha of Syria and Egypt; for this made certain that the Czar would strike, even if alone.

So in 1826 Canning came to an agreement with Russia, and France joined to enforce an armistice and ensure the freedom of Greece from Turkish rule. The three Powers backed-up their efforts by sending naval forces to Greek waters, and in September 1827 their warships assembled off the island of Zante in the Adriatic. The Russian division was commanded by Rear-Admiral de Heyden, the British by Vice-Admiral Sir Edward Codrington, and the French by Rear-Admiral Gauthier de Rigny. Codrington, as the senior in rank (he also happened to have the most ships), took command of the combined fleet of ten ships-of-the-line, ten frigates and half-a-dozen brigs and schooners.

The Allied force was vastly outnumbered by the Turkish and Egyptian ships, which totalled sixty-five, but only three of these were line-of-battle ships. There were, however, nineteen frigates, and the weight of metal amounted to 1,962 guns against the 1,294 of the Allies.

The Turkish commander-in-chief, Ibrahim Pasha, had anchored his fleet in the Bay of Navarino, on the west coast of the Peloponnese – not far from where the Battle of Lepanto had been fought. His ships were drawn up in three lines in a horseshoe formation extending from the Navarino fort on the mainland to the battery on the island of Sphacteria. On 25 September Codrington and de Rigny had a meeting with Ibrahim Pasha to inform him of the Allied offer of mediation, which had already been accepted by the Greeks. The Turkish commander gave a verbal agreement that his ships

RIGHT Ibrahim Pasha, the Turkish commander-in-chief.

FAR RIGHT Vice-Admiral Sir Edward Codrington, the Allied commander-in-chief at Navarino.

ABOVE Lord Cochrane, commander of the Greek naval division.

ABOVE RIGHT Rear-admiral Gauthier de Rigny, the commander of the French division.

ABOVE, FAR RIGHT Rear-Admiral Count de Heyden, the commander of the Russian division under Vice-Admiral Sir Edward Codrington.

would not leave Navarino until a reply to the Allied proposition had been received from the Sultan. The Allied fleet therefore withdrew, leaving two frigates to keep watch on Navarino.

It seemed that a settlement might be reached, but at this point the Greek naval division came into the picture. Its presence was reported in the Gulf of Patras. The commander was Lord Cochrane, an audacious leader of light craft who had previously organized the navy of Chile when that country was fighting for freedom. Ibrahim Pasha objected to the near presence of this Greek force at such a moment and sent some of his ships, under the command of Petrona Bey, to demand Cochrane's withdrawal. But Codrington, with his flagship, the 84-gun *Asia*, and three frigates intercepted Petrona Bey south of the Gulf of Patras and told him not to proceed. Petrona Bey turned back, but another Turkish detachment of some fifteen vessels was met later, proceeding with the same purpose; these, too, withdrew when Codrington barred their way.

In the meantime the Turkish forces had been burning and plundering the Greek coastal town of Pylos and devastating the interior. Codrington therefore decided, after consultation with the Russian and French commanders, to put pressure on Ibrahim Pasha and to stand into Navarino Bay with the

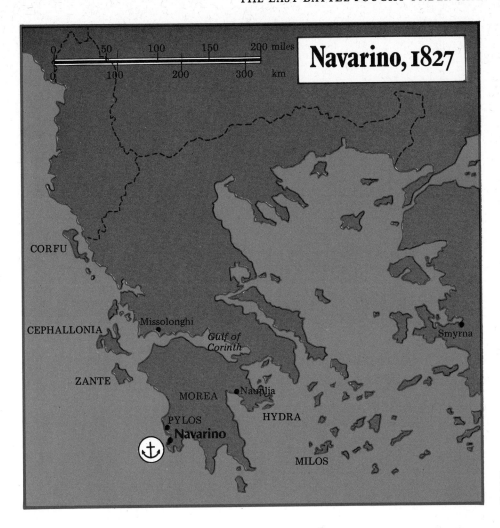

BELOW The Allied fleet entering
Navarino Bay at the start of
the battle.

Allied fleet. As the Turks had already given way before a small demonstration of force, there was no reason to suppose that they would provoke a full-scale action.

It was about noon on 20 October when Codrington sailed into the bay, leading the fleet in the *Asia*, aided by a slight following wind. He went between the Navarino fort and the eastern shore of the little island of Sphacteria, where the Turks had mounted a battery. He was in effect putting his head into a noose, for the Turkish and Egyptian ships were still moored in a horseshoe formation which barred the exit from the bay on the other side of Sphacteria, while the guns of the Navarino fort and the island battery commanded the narrow entrance through which the Allied fleet was passing. There were more shore batteries at the head of the bay, protecting Ibrahim's ships. Codrington was either supremely confident or extremely foolhardy; perhaps both.

However, there was no reaction from the other side as the Allied ships sailed slowly in and anchored as prearranged, except for the Russian ships becalmed in the rear; what little wind there was had suddenly fallen. The *Asia* dropped anchor near Ibrahim's flagship, and the *Sirène*, de Rigny's flagship, anchored even closer to the Egyptian flagship.

For a time, nothing happened. Whatever the object of the exercise, it took an unexpected turn when the *Dartmouth*, a 44-gun frigate, sent off a boat with an officer to request one of the Turkish fireships to keep her distance. Someone fired at the boat and killed the officer. The *Dartmouth*'s captain promptly

BELOW The battle of Navarino.

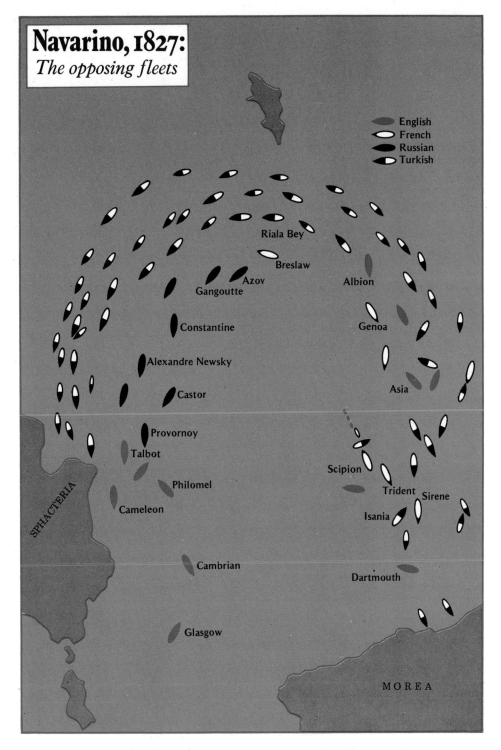

Navarino, 1827:
The opposing fleets

English
French
Russian
Turkish

Riala Bey
Breslaw
Azov
Gangoutte
Albion
Constantine
Genoa
Alexandre Newsky
Castor
Asia
Provornoy
Talbot
Philomel
Scipion
Cameleon
Trident
Sirene
Isania
SPHACTERIA
Cambrian
Dartmouth
Glasgow
MOREA

ordered his men to give covering fire to the returning boat's crew. Then, like an echo spreading round the bay, firing broke out from ship after ship. The Egyptian frigate *Irania* opened fire on the *Sirène*, which ran out her guns to reply. The 74-gun *Albion*, nearest to the head of the bay and somewhat isolated from the rest of the British squadron, attacked and boarded a Turkish ship. The French *Scipion* was almost set alight by an unmanned, blazing Turkish fireship, warding it off just in time but causing it to drift down to the *Daphne* ... which directed it into a cluster of Turkish and Egyptian vessels.

RIGHT The French frigate
La Provence lying in Navarino Bay
two days after the battle, having
been left behind to complete repairs
to her main-mast.

A couple of shore batteries opened up, while the ships of the Allied force tried to get under way. The fighting was so confused that no coherent description of it has ever been possible. It lasted less than an hour, and in that time Ibrahim's fleet was overwhelmed. Or rather, his ships set fire to themselves in the hope of destroying any enemy ship that drew near. In this way the *Irania*, which had fought the *Sirène* all the time, blew up before the French ship had drawn off, and the shock of the explosion brought down the latter's mizzen. Only one Turkish ship struck her colours, a frigate which was disabled by the French *Trident*.

The casualties were heavy for such a short action, but the fighting had been at close quarters. The total of Allied wounded was nearly five hundred and the death roll was seventy-five British, fifty-nine Russians and forty-three French. No one knows how many were killed and wounded on the other side.

The Turks and Egyptians seemed set on continuing the destruction of their own ships; the following day they were beaching and burning those that were still afloat, and Codrington sent envoys to explain that it was not his intention to destroy or capture their fleet. The Allies had been fired on first, and had replied . . . and would do so again, if necessary, but not if the Turks respected the agreement and kept the truce.

The final touch to the whole affair was when the Greeks – for whom, after all, the European powers had been fighting – sent their privateers to stop and search European merchant ships that came within sight.

What folly it all was! Codrington was recalled to London and relieved of his command. De Rigny, though, was promoted to Vice-Admiral and given a title. The end of the affair was as confused as the beginning.

9 The Coming of the Ironclads

Hampton Roads, 1862

The American Civil War gave the country's naval engineers and officers opportunities to play a leading part in the evolution of sea warfare, which had recently seen great changes with the introduction of the shell-gun and the advances in steam power.

At the outbreak of the war, the Confederate States had no navy to oppose the five Union ships which were blockading the Chesapeake and the river approaches to Norfolk, Virginia. This was the frontier between the two sides, and their shore batteries faced each other across the wide bay. So a scuttled wooden frigate (the USS *Merrimack*, scuttled by the Union when Virginia went over to the Confederates) was raised from Norfolk harbour, in July 1861, and work was begun to convert her into an ironclad, a ship cased with plates of protective armour. The five Union ships were all wooden, and an ironclad with powerful armament should be able to eliminate them without much difficulty.

Work on the ex-*Merrimack* went on for eight months and at the end she appeared as a cumbersome monstrosity of a ship. She had a draught of twenty-three feet and only two feet of freeboard, and could make no more than five knots. On the other hand, what protection and weight of armament! The *Virginia*, as the ironclad was named, had three 8-inch guns and two 6-inch, two 7-inch swivel guns and a heavy steel beak or lance at the stem. Her command was given to a Captain Buchanan, who had been the first Commander of the Naval Academy at Annapolis before going over to the Confederacy. He had some difficulty in completing his crew, but eventually local seamen and volunteers from the army brought the number to 350.

The Union ships were still maintaining the blockade, but the *Virginia* had a race against time in order to destroy them. News had been received that a formidable adversary was being constructed at New York. This was the *Monitor*, the first ship to be conceived and built as an ironclad. She represented a revolution in shipbuilding. The super-structure was reduced to a minimum, so that the ship's shortened outline gave little help to enemy gun-layers; and there was hardly more than one foot of freeboard. But the ship drew only twelve feet of water, as compared with the *Virginia*'s twenty-three. Her armament consisted of two 11-inch guns – the largest calibre of the time – both in a turret nine feet high and twenty feet in diameter and which revolved on a circular brass rail inserted in the deck; its pivot went right down to the keel. The turret was protected with one-inch iron plates and its roof covered with iron nails. It weighed one hundred and forty tons, and was turned by an auxiliary steam-driven engine.

The *Monitor* was launched at the beginning of March 1862 and left New York for the Chesapeake on 6 March under the command of Lt-Commander John L. Worden and towed by two wooden steamships; there was no question of the ironclad sailing the open sea under her own power. This maiden voyage was almost her last; the very next day, when off the mouth

THIS PAGE The victorious crew
(*above*) and officers (*right*) of the
Union ironclad *Monitor*, a few
months after the action at
Hampton Roads.

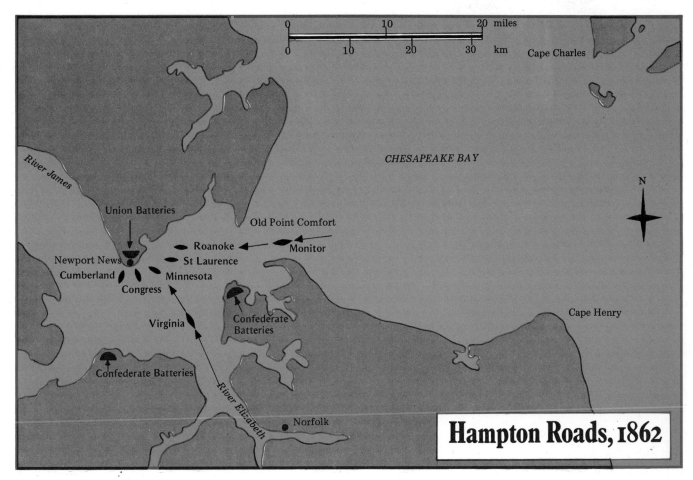

CHESAPEAKE BAY

Cape Charles

Old Point Comfort

Union Batteries

Newport News

Cumberland

Congress

Virginia

Roanoke

St Laurence

Minnesota

Monitor

Confederate Batteries

Confederate Batteries

Norfolk

River James

River Elizabeth

Cape Henry

N

Hampton Roads, 1862

of the Delaware River, she met bad weather and was soon in difficulty. She was shipping water everywhere, through the funnel and the air-vents. The nightmare voyage ended on the afternoon of 8 March when the *Monitor* rounded Cape Charles and reached the sheltered waters of Chesapeake Bay – to the sounds of cannon-fire.

That very morning Captain Buchanan had cast off at Norfolk and the *Virginia* had been towed down the river to attack the blockading ships on the other side of the bay. These were the 50-gun, screw-driven frigates *Minnesota*, *Roanoke* and *Congress* (of the same class as the ex-*Merrimack*), the 52-gun sailing frigate *St Lawrence* and the 24-gun sloop *Cumberland*, all under the command of Admiral Goldsborough, USN. Once out of the river, the *Virginia* headed across the bay under her own power – for the first time. Her crew had had no firing practice either, so both ship and crew were to be tried out while under fire. The *Virginia* quickly proved herself a clumsy ship to handle; the simplest manœuvre took half an hour to carry out!

But the Union ships were not expecting to have to fight that day; washing was hanging out to dry on the decks, and the *Cumberland*'s captain was ashore. The *Virginia* opened fire on the *Congress* at 1,500 yards, and her superiority at once became obvious. The shot from the *Congress*'s 25-pounders ricocheted off the *Virginia*'s armoured plating, whereas the latter's fire smashed the oak hull of the Union frigate. Buchanan then turned his attention to the *Cumberland*, ramming her on the starboard bow and crushing the hull like an eggshell, at the same time firing his bow-chaser and killing ten men. The *Cumberland* began to sink so quickly that she threatened to drag the ironclad down with her.

The *Virginia* turned to finish off the *Congress*, which, however, managed to run aground where the ironclad could not get close enough to board her. But from a distance of 150 yards Buchanan sent in shell after shell. The bombardment put all the guns out of action, killed the captain and forced the first lieutenant to strike his colours. The *Virginia* was in the process of securing her prize and taking the prisoners aboard when Union troops arrived and opened fire from the shore, soon supported by their shore batteries. Buchanan hurriedly recalled the prize-crew and pounded the *Congress* with red-hot shot to set her alight. Then he was badly wounded in the leg, and Lieutenant Jones took over command.

The other three Union ships had gone aground while trying to reach the scene of the action. After endeavouring for three hours to get within range of one or the other, the *Virginia* returned across the bay as darkness was falling and anchored under the protection of the Confederate batteries. She had destroyed two enemy ships and damaged a third, and inflicted two hundred and fifty casualties; yet only twenty-one of her crew had been killed or wounded, and the sole damage was a gash in her bows from ramming the *Cumberland*. The news of the victory was joyfully telegraphed all over the Southern States.

However, the battle was not yet over. Soon after the *Virginia* had withdrawn across the bay, the *Monitor* steamed into Hampton Roads and stopped in a position where she could protect the stranded *Minnesota*. The flames from the burning *Congress* were casting a flickering light over the scene. She

OPPOSITE TOP The battle of Hampton Roads – a view from the shore.

OPPOSITE BOTTOM The sinking of the Union sloop *Cumberland* by the Confederate ironclad *Virginia*.

ABOVE The silver medal struck
to commemorate the first battle
between ironclad ships.

blew up just before midnight, and then an uneasy silence settled over the dark waters.

As day was beginning to break, the men on watch in the *Monitor* made out the *Virginia* heading across the bay towards the *Minnesota*. Battle was joined at once, and the *Virginia* found it a very different proposition from the previous day. The superiority of the *Monitor* quickly became evident; she was much the more manageable ship, especially in these shallow waters. But neither ironclad suffered from the gunfire of the other; even the *Monitor*'s 11-inch made no impression on the *Virginia*'s protective armour. Lieutenant Jones then decided to ram his adversary as Captain Buchanan had done so successfully to the *Cumberland*, and headed at full speed towards the *Monitor*. But Lt-Commander Worden swung his ship away just in time, and the *Virginia* only caught her a glancing blow which was more harmful to the already damaged bows of the aggressor.

Finding he could do nothing to the *Monitor*, Jones turned his guns on the *Minnesota*, which eventually caught fire. But while manoeuvring to avoid the *Monitor*, which had come to the help of the frigate, the *Virginia* took the ground and seemed at the mercy of the enemy ironclad. However, a lucky shot struck the slits of the *Monitor*'s armoured control-cabin, temporarily blinding her captain. The helmsman was left without orders for a while and continued on course, which took the ship away from the *Virginia*. Churning up the mud, the latter succeeded in getting into deeper water and promptly retired across the bay.

Thus ended the first battle between ironclads, in which protective armour had the advantage over missiles. Both ships had received a great many hits; but the only damage caused to the *Monitor* was by the hit on her control-cabin, while the *Virginia* – on which the marks of forty-one hits were counted – had only a few armoured plates fractured.

After this action, sea warfare was never the same again.

10 An American Duel at Dawn

Cherbourg, 1864

One day in August 1862 a crew arrived to join 'No. 290', a new three-masted barque with two auxiliary steam-engines built at Birkenhead, England, for, it was said, the Khedive of Egypt. In fact the agent who had arranged the contract held credentials from President Davis of the Confederate States of America. The crew was a pack of adventurers; 'a hundred and ten of the most reckless boozers from the Liverpool pubs', was how their captain later described them. But the officers were American, supporters of the Confederacy, and a couple of days later when they took the barque to sea for her final trials they 'forgot' to return to port. On 18 August the barque put in at the Azores and was there joined by the *Agrippine* of London, bringing the guns and ammunition and a great quantity of coal. Two days later Captain Raphael Semmes arrived to take over his command. The Portuguese authorities turned a blind eye on the conversion of 'No. 290' into an armed raider. She was armed with eight guns: six 32-pounders, one 8-inch and 'the only successful rifled 100-pounder yet produced in England,' claimed her captain. On 24 August he took her out to sea, mustered the crew and read out to them his commission from the President of the Confederate States to the command of the CSS *Alabama*. He then set out on a voyage of destruction unparalleled in modern naval annals.

Raphael Semmes was, like his first lieutenant, John McIntosh Kell, one of the 320 officers who had resigned from the Union Navy. He was in his fifties, a slightly built man with waxed, pointed moustaches. 'Old Beeswax', as he came to be called among the crew, had a disarming gentleness; he was a deeply religious man but with an almost Judaic venomous desire for retribution against his enemies. He had already gained considerable experience of raiding Federal shipping, having commanded the converted mail-packet *Sumter* for seven months and destroyed seventeen Union merchantmen during her long cruise in the Atlantic. Now, on leaving the Azores with the *Alabama*, in three months he captured twenty-six enemy ships, ransoming six of them and burning the others after taking the crews prisoner.

Semmes then wisely transferred his activities to the South Atlantic and the Indian Ocean. But the *Alabama*'s score increased less rapidly than in earlier months, because Union ships were being transferred to foreign flags at a great rate; their owners dared not send them to sea under their own flag, such was the menace of the *Alabama* and other commerce raiders. In the summer of 1864, after twenty months of scouring the seas, Semmes brought the *Alabama* back to Europe, capturing two more ships in the Atlantic and bringing his total to seventy-one. On 11 June he was off Cherbourg, where he asked permission to enter harbour for a much-needed overhaul.

The French vice-admiral pointed out that Cherbourg was a naval dockyard and that 'it would be better to go to Le Havre, as the government might not give permission for repairs to a belligerent ship in one of its own dockyards'.

ABOVE Captain Raphael Semmes, the commander of the Confederate sloop-of-war *Alabama*.

BELOW John McIntosh Kell, First Lieutenant on the *Alabama*.

ABOVE AND OPPOSITE The Union
man-of-war USS *Kearsage* sinking
the Confederate ship *Alabama*.

He would have to refer Semmes's request to Paris. Meanwhile the *Alabama* was allowed to enter harbour. Permission was given for Semmes to land the thirty-seven prisoners he had on board and for his crew to go ashore.

Unfortunately for Semmes, telegraphic communications existed in Europe. A Union man-of-war, the USS *Kearsage*, was lying at Flushing. The United States Consul in Paris got a message through to her captain, and three days after the *Alabama* had moored at Cherbourg the *Kearsage* arrived outside the harbour.

Captain John Winslow of the *Kearsage*, a balding man and blind in his right eye, only two years younger than Semmes, had been his colleague in the days before the Civil War; but there was no thought of friendship in Winslow's mind now. Semmes did not keep him waiting for long. Faced with the alternative of internment or going out to fight, he sent a challenge to his adversary, gave his ship's papers and forty-five chronometers (souvenirs of some of his victims) into the safe-keeping of the port authorities, and left harbour at dawn on 19 June, a Sunday.

The imminent prospect of this sea-fight had naturally caused great excitement on both sides of the Channel. An English yacht, the *Deerhound*, chanced to appear in the area; what was more, an excursion train brought twelve hundred Parisians to watch the spectacle from the heights of Cherbourg. They were not disappointed.

The two American ships were fairly evenly matched. The *Alabama* had

ABOVE Survivors from the *Alabama* row ashore as their ship goes down.

eight guns and a crew of 149; the *Kearsage*, manned by 163 men, carried seven guns, but two were 11-inch. Both ships were of about the same tonnage and length. However, the *Kearsage* was staunch and well-built, a man-of-war in fighting trim. The *Alabama* was more lightly constructed, made for flight and speed; she had been halfway round the world and was badly in need of an overhaul. Moreover, Captain Winslow had improvised some protection for his engines by spreading anchor-chains over the sides, and had then dissimilated this by covering them with planking. Later, after the action, Semmes was most indignant about this, accusing Winslow of taking unfair advantage.

The *Alabama* opened fire first, from two thousand yards, and the shot cut some of the *Kearsage*'s rigging. For eighteen minutes the action continued without casualties. Then a shell from the *Alabama* passed through the starboard bulwarks of the Union ship and exploded on the quarter-deck, wounding three members of a gun-crew. But this was the only effective hit made by the *Alabama*. It was a curious sort of fight, for each ship endeavoured to rake the other; they moved in two concentric circles, firing at each other and drawing ever closer, until they were little more than six hundred yards apart. The shooting from the *Kearsage* was the more accurate and effective – hardly surprising, considering the composition of the *Alabama*'s crew. Only fourteen of the 370 shots from the *Alabama* made hits on the *Kearsage*; one of

LEFT The English yacht *Deerhound* rescuing survivors from the *Alabama*.

these, from the 100-pounder, struck the sternpost but failed to explode. Had it done so, the *Kearsage* would have foundered fifteen minutes after the fight started.

It raged for an hour, and then a lucky shot from one of the *Kearsage*'s 11-inch guns put the raider's engines out of action. The *Alabama* had received her death blow; water was pouring in through holes in her side at such a rate that the fires in her furnaces were extinguished. 'Cease firing', Semmes ordered Lieutenant Kell, 'shorten sail and haul down the colours. It will never do in this nineteenth century for us to go down and the decks covered with our gallant wounded.'

All the *Alabama*'s boats were damaged except one; this was lowered and the wounded placed in it to be rowed to the *Kearsage*. With them went the master's mate, who announced that the *Alabama* had surrendered and was rapidly sinking; he asked that boats be sent immediately to rescue the crew. The *Kearsage* herself had only two boats that were not disabled; these were lowered and went to the rescue. Standing by within hailing distance was the yacht *Deerhound*, owned by a Mr John Lancaster. Winslow yelled to him, 'For God's sake do what you can to save them!' The yacht immediately steamed towards the sinking *Alabama*.

Her mainmast broke as she went down by the stern. The *Kearsage* rescued about seventy of her crew, some of them wounded, and these were put into hospital at Cherbourg. The *Deerhound* landed Semmes, who had been hauled from the water, and thirty-nine of his officers and men at Southampton that evening – much to the indignation of Captain Winslow, who later complained at the *Deerhound* 'taking our prisoners off'.

As the yacht sailed up the Solent, some of the *Alabama*'s officers began to express their appreciation to Lancaster. 'Gentlemen', he replied, 'you have no need to give me any special thanks. I should have done exactly the same for the other people if they had needed it.'

11 The Russians' Long Haul to Disaster

Tsushima, 1905

Hostilities between Russia and Japan were opened in February 1904 when the Japanese High Command made a surprise attack before a state of war had been officially declared – as at Pearl Harbor thirty-seven years later. A little before midnight on 8 February a Japanese flotilla of torpedo-boats swooped down upon the Russian warships lying peacefully in the roadstead outside the narrow entrance of Port Arthur, crippled two battleships and a cruiser, and entirely altered the balance of naval power in the Far East.

The Japanese followed up their torpedo attack by blockading Port Arthur and strengthened the siege by landing troops and guns which were able to direct artillery fire on the anchorage. The fate of the remaining Russian ships at Port Arthur was now sealed, unless reinforcements could reach them in time.

The Russian Home Fleet was divided between the Baltic and the Black Sea. The Baltic squadron was needed there, and the Black Sea squadron was not allowed, under the Treaty of London of 1870, to pass through the Dardanelles. So the Minister of Marine decided to form a new squadron which would be sent out to the Far East to restore the balance of power. There were five powerful battleships under construction in the shipyards; by great effort four were ready by the middle of September 1904.

The command of this second Far East squadron was entrusted to the Deputy Chief of Naval Staff, Admiral Rojestvensky. He was fifty-six and had served in the navy since 1865, but with only short periods at sea: an excellent staff officer, intelligent and firm, but lacking imagination. The squadron finally sailed from the Baltic on 14 October, Rojestvensky flying his flag in the 12-inch battleship *Knias Souvaroff*. She was one of the four new battleships, each of 13,500 tons with armour-plating nine inches thick, armed with four 12-inch guns and twelve 6-inch, and carrying a crew of about 750. There were three smaller battleships in the squadron, though two were armed with twin-turrets of 12-inch guns, and three elderly armoured cruisers with 8-inch guns. Altogether Rojestvensky commanded forty-five ships including transports and two hospital ships. It was a formidable force – on paper. But there had been no time to work up the new battleships and the crews had received no training – there would be time enough on the voyage! A voyage which was bound to end with a major naval action in Japanese waters against an enemy who was fresh and rested, and having had months in which to prepare.

It is almost eighteen thousand miles from the Baltic to Vladivostock by way of the Cape of Good Hope; and there was not a single Russian base in the whole distance. It would have been better for Russia to have cut her losses and not prolonged a war that had begun so badly for her. That was very likely what Admiral Sinovie Petrovitch Rojestvensky often thought during his long

THIS PAGE Two views of the
Russo-Japanese war by Toshikide.
Another Russian ship is sunk
(*above*) and (*left*) a caricature
of Nicholas II.

voyage from the Baltic. It was what all logical persons and naval officers everywhere thought.

On 3 November the Russian ships reached Tangiers – not then an international zone – and Rojestvensky had no difficulty over coaling from the waiting colliers, which had been chartered from the Hamburg-Amerika Line. The Sultan of Morocco was officially unaware that a state of war existed between Russia and Japan, and so felt that he could ignore the international conventions under which neutral powers were forbidden to give shelter for more than twenty-four hours to the warships of belligerent nations. The squadron stayed three days in the roadstead, and here Rojestvensky divided his force. The two smallest battleships, three light cruisers and the destroyers were sent eastward via Suez under the command of Rear-Admiral Folkersam, while Rojestvensky took the heavier ships and the auxiliaries southward to the Cape. A rendezvous was fixed at Madagascar, and from there the whole squadron would cross the Indian Ocean together.

Folkersam was first to reach the rendezvous, Nossi-Bé Island, an out-of-the-way place with a good anchorage, off the north-west coast of Madagascar. Rojestvensky arrived a week or so later, in mid-January 1905, having had many difficulties over coaling his ships and having experienced a long succession of mechanical breakdowns. 'Our long voyage was a prolonged and despairing struggle with boilers that burst and engines that broke down,' wrote one of the staff officers. 'On one occasion, practically every ship's boilers had to be relit in the space of twenty-four hours.'

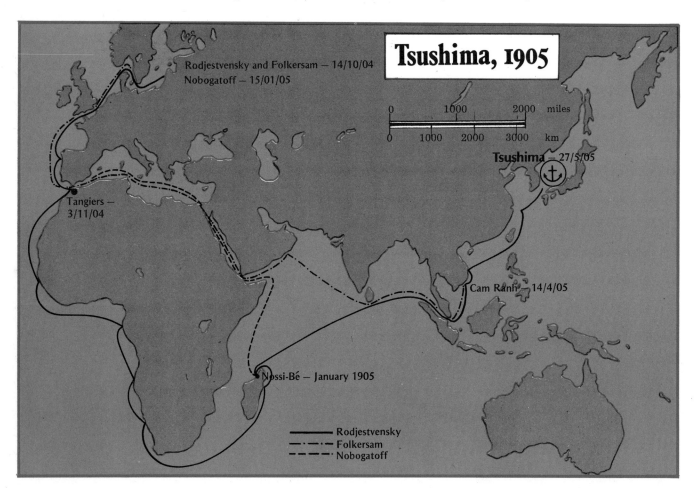

LEFT Rear-Admiral Nebogatoff, commander of the 'sink-by-themselves class'.

Folkersam's ships, too, were all in bad shape and required repairs which meant they would have to remain at the anchorage for at least a fortnight. And Folkersam had received news of the capitulation of Port Arthur on 2 January 1905, after the few remaining Russian ships had been scuttled; this removed all hope of any aid from that quarter when Rojestvensky's squadron reached Japanese waters – if it ever did. To crown all, news came from St Petersburg that a division under the command of Rear-Admiral Nebogatoff was being sent to join Rojestvensky's squadron. The Naval Staff had wanted to add these old, worn-out ships – their crews called them the 'sink-by-themselves class' – to Rojestvensky's squadron before he sailed from the Baltic, and he thought he had succeeded in discarding them. They would be more of a hindrance than anything; Rojestvensky would have preferred going into action with a smaller but better-balanced squadron than he had already.

In the hope of eluding these undesirable reinforcements, he sailed from Nossi-Bé as soon as he could. He passed through the Malacca Straits on 8 April and six days later dropped anchor at Cam Ranh, on the coast of French Indo-China – a passage of 4,500 miles from Madagascar, the longest ever made between one port and another by a coal-fuelled squadron.

Rojestvensky received strict instructions from St Petersburg to await Nebogatoff and his ships before proceeding any further. Thus began a fortnight or so of waiting, losing what little morale the crews still had. On

ABOVE LEFT Nebogatoff's flagship, the ancient battleship *Imperator Nikolai I*.

ABOVE RIGHT *Orel*, one of the four modern battleships in the Russian fleet.

BELOW Admiral Togo, the Japanese commander-in-chief.

25 May Rojestvensky was off Shanghai with his combined force. To have got so far was an exploit worthy of better reward. . . .

Rojestvensky had the choice of three routes by which to penetrate the Sea of Japan and reach Vladivostock. The obvious route was through the Straits of Korea; it was the shortest and gave more room for manœuvre, being as wide as the North Sea between Harwich and the Hook of Holland. It was also the most likely position for the Japanese fleet to concentrate. But there was now an inevitability about the encounter, emphasized by a gloomy fatalism on the Russian side.

Rojestvensky did what he could. He detached most of his auxiliary ships, sending them to anchor in the mouth of the Yangtse, then sailed slowly northward on 26 May, timing his advance so as not to pass through the Straits at night, for fear of a torpedo attack. He sent two cruisers toward the east coast of Japan in an attempt to persuade the enemy that his whole squadron was intending to pass into the Pacific and round the Japanese islands, but the trick failed.

At daybreak on 27 May there was a thick haze in the Straits with patches of fog here and there, and a fresh south-west wind was building up a heavy sea. The spirits of the Russians rose a little. They were then sailing in two columns and making for the passage between Tsushima Island and the Japanese mainland. A Japanese scouting cruiser sighted them briefly through the mist; there was no need for her to run back to the fleet with her news, as would have happened in former wars, for she was equipped with wireless. She sent a coded signal to Admiral Togo's flagship: 'Enemy fleet in sight in square 203 apparently making for the eastern channel.'

Twice during the morning, Japanese light cruisers appeared out of the thinning mist on the Russians' port beam, steered on a parallel course for a while, then withdrew after making this reconnaissance. The Russians, who were keeping radio silence, rightly concluded that they had watchful enemies all round them, ushering them towards the battle squadron waiting ahead.

The Japanese commander-in-chief, Admiral Togo, flying his flag in the battleship *Mikasa*, was in fact barring the way to the Russians. He had with him six 12-inch battleships and six armoured cruisers, a division of protected cruisers and a flotilla of destroyers. The whole force cruised slowly southward past the island of Tsushima in the middle of the Straits. At 13.45 the enemy ships came in sight to the south-west. Flags fluttered up the signal halliards of the *Mikasa*, and the ships' crews got the message: 'The rise or fall of the Empire depends upon today's battle. Let every man do his utmost.'

LEFT Admiral Togo's flagship, the battleship *Mikasa*.

Rojestvensky had hoisted the signal 'Steer north twenty-three degrees east for Vladivostock'. It was to remain flying until the end. Never before had two such powerful fleets met in battle. But the result was almost a fore-gone conclusion. The Japanese possessed new and better guns, and during the past months there had been exercises at sea and target practice to bring every ship and man up to the mark. Their battle squadron could manœuvre at fifty per cent greater speed than the enemy, whose weed-covered bottom-plates handicapped even the newest ships.

The battle opened with Togo's heavy ships turning eastward to 'cross the

ABOVE A contemporary
impression of the
Japanese attack.

T' to the Russians, while his light forces swung south to attack their rear. As
the *Mikasa* led the Japanese line in its turning movement, Rojestvensky
swung round to starboard and opened fire at the – then – astonishing range
of 9,000 yards. Togo waited until within 6,500 yards, and then his ships
concentrated their fire on the flagships of the two leading divisions, the
Souvaroff and *Ossliabya*. The Japanese gunners soon found their aim, with
disastrous consequences to the *Ossliabya*. Blazing from stem to stern, and
with a gaping hole from three hits close together, she began to sink and disappeared at 14.25, only twenty minutes after the opening of the action. She
was the first steam battleship ever sunk by gunfire. Three destroyers picked
up some two hundred of her crew.

Five minutes later a shell wrecked the after-turret of the *Souvaroff*, then
her foremast went and two funnels crashed down. Her steering gear was
disabled and she drifted from her station at the head of the line, fires spreading
rapidly throughout her length. The 12-inch shells of the Japanese were
demonstrating their frightful powers of destruction. The big gun had proved
itself at sea.

'The *Souvaroff* no longer looked like a ship,' says a Japanese account. 'After
the first twenty minutes of the action the Russians seemed to go all to pieces
and their shooting became wild and almost harmless.'

When the *Souvaroff* swerved out of line, the *Imperator Alexander III*
became the leading ship. Her captain tried to break through to the northward,
only to receive the concentrated fire of several enemy ships. She turned east-

ward, followed by her consorts in a straggling line, and then drifted out of her place leaking badly and with her upper works ablaze. Soon afterwards she capsized and sank. There were only four survivors.

The *Borodino* now had the dangerous post at the head of the line. She steamed eastward for nearly an hour, followed by Togo on a parallel course, the Japanese fire only slackening when mist and smoke obscured its targets. Before this, the Japanese light cruisers commanded by Rear-Admiral Dewa had worked round to the southward of the Russians and were driving the transports and their escorts northeast towards the main force, sinking two ships, badly damaging the cruiser *Svietlana* and setting several other vessels on fire. But the Japanese did not have it all their own way. The rear-admiral's cruiser was hit below the waterline and was in such danger of sinking that he handed over command to Captain Uriu and steered for the Japanese coast.

By 17.00 the Russians were huddled together in a confused crowd, the light cruisers, transports and remaining heavy ships, assailed from the east by Togo and harried from the south by Uriu. Away to the westward lay the disabled and burning *Souvaroff*, but with her flag still flying. Her captain had been blown to pieces, Rojestvensky had been twice wounded and was unconscious. Most of the guns were out of action, but a 6-inch quick-firer and a few lighter guns kept firing and drove off the first attempt of Japanese destroyers to dash in and sink her. Still there was no thought of surrender.

LEFT The battleship *Alexander III* with her crew, only four of whom survived when she was sunk at Tsushima.

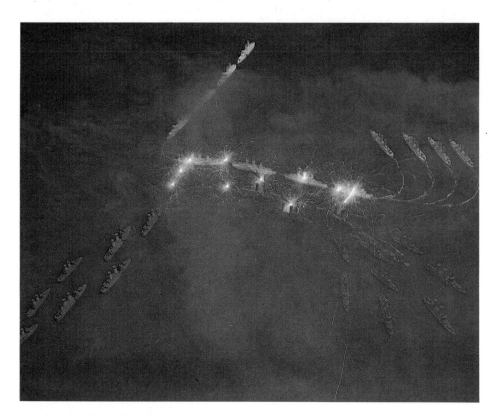

RIGHT Two plans of the battle of Tsushima.

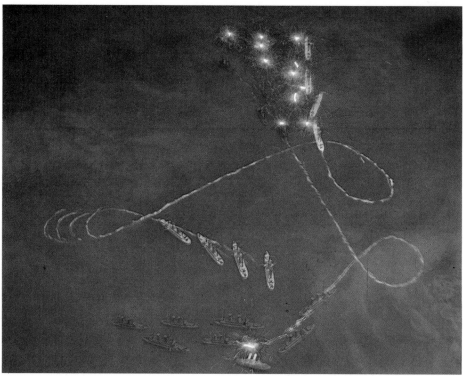

Her remaining crew fought with dogged Russian courage to the last. A Russian destroyer, the *Buiny*, managed to get alongside and took off Rojestvensky and a few others. The admiral revived enough to send a message to Nebogatoff (Folkersam had died at sea two days before the battle), telling him to take over command and repeating the order 'head for Vladivostock' as though nothing had happened in the meantime. The gallant

Souvaroff stayed afloat for another hour, her last gun still firing, until some torpedo-boats sent her to the bottom.

At about 17.30 Nebogatoff managed to force his way northward out of the press with a straggle of ships which included the remaining two modern battleships, the *Borodino* and *Orel*. Togo's heavy ships pursued them for a while, and the 12-inch battleship *Fuji* scored a direct hit on the magazines of the *Borodino*, which blew up. Her keel remained above water for a few minutes, then suddenly disappeared.

The twilight was deepening into night, and Togo called off the chase to enable his torpedo-boats to operate, though there was still a choppy sea. The Japanese heavy ships were ordered to steam northeast during the night and to rendezvous at dawn at a point just south of Matsu-shima island, about one hundred and fifty miles north of Tsushima.

Meanwhile Nebogatoff's flagship, the ancient battleship *Imperator Nikolai I*, held a northerly course followed by the *Orel* and an assortment of cruisers, some limping along and others already in a sinking condition. A few light cruisers and transports had escaped southward and were heading back to Shanghai. The remaining Russian survivors were steaming slowly about the Sea of Japan, some isolated, some in improvised divisions, all bearing many marks of the battle.

Soon after 20.00 the first Japanese attack by torpedo-boats went in. Several ships were hit but kept afloat. The chief effect of the attack was to disperse Nebogatoff's ships in all directions. At about midnight the small battleship *Navarin* was hit by two torpedoes; leaking badly, she struggled on northward. A cruiser was hit astern and limped along throughout the night, only to sink at daybreak. The Russians managed to sink a couple of the torpedo-boats and to damage two others; as dawn began to whiten the sky, the torpedo flotilla drew off.

The action off Tsushima and the running fight during the night had taken the ships one hundred and fifty miles. Never before had a naval battle spread over such distance. Steaming steadily through the night, Togo's battle squadron had passed eastward of the scattered Russians, and daybreak on 28 May found the Japanese still barring their way to Vladivostock. Togo's light cruisers and destroyers coming up from the south sighted the *Nikolai* and four other Russians – all that remained as a cohesive fighting force – soon after sunrise. These ships were little damaged, but they saw a score and more enemies appear from all points of the compass, battleships and armoured cruisers among them, which opened fire at long range. The Russians could not reply effectively; in any case, they had little ammunition left. Nebogatoff did not hesitate for long. He hoisted the international signal of surrender.

One of the ships with him, the cruiser *Izumrud*, managed to slip away and made at all speed for Vladivostock; unfortunately her coal bunkers were almost empty and she just failed to reach there. Her captain made Vladimir Bay, the extreme limit of Russian-held territory, with only ten tons of coal left; but in the dark the ship struck a reef. Fearing the arrival of Japanese warships in the morning, the captain landed his crew and blew up the ship.

The remaining Russian units in the Sea of Japan tried to escape the net, but few succeeded. One by one, they were rounded up and captured or sunk. The *Navarin* was still limping northward on the afternoon of the twenty-eighth when she was found and attacked by four destroyers. Her crew fought back until repeated hits sent her to the bottom; there were three survivors.

Admiral Togo on the bridge of his flagship, the *Mikasa*.

Rojestvensky and his surviving staff officers were captured on board the destroyer *Biedovy*, to which they had transferred when the *Buiny* broke down during the night. Only three of all the ships which Rojestvensky had led into the Sea of Japan finally arrived at Vladivostock: two destroyers and a light cruiser.

The Japanese had one armoured cruiser and two light cruisers badly damaged, and six or seven destroyers were in need of repairs. The number of Japanese killed was under six hundred, but six thousand Russians had perished in this battle which determined the outcome of the Russo-Japanese War. Three weeks later, a peace treaty was signed. Japan obtained Port Arthur and the southern half of Sakhalin, the long narrow island off the coast of Siberia and just north of Japan.

Tsushima created a precedent which made a deep impression on navies the world over; henceforth, sea warfare became more implacable. It was still known for troops or a besieged garrison to surrender, whereas a warship, a squadron, no longer struck to the enemy. Yet many great sea-captains in the era of sail had done so, without their future career or reputation suffering; it was not then considered dishonourable to strike one's colours after putting up a valiant fight. But since Tsushima, few indeed are the captains who have surrendered their ship or even tried to save their crew by taking to the boats after scuttling a vessel no longer capable of fighting.

12 Where the Germans Deserved Better

The Falklands, 1914

At the Battle of Coronel, off the coast of Chile, on 1 November 1914 a British squadron of obsolete cruisers was almost wiped out in less than an hour by a crack German squadron of modern cruisers commanded by Vice-Admiral Graf von Spee. When news of this crushing defeat reached the Admiralty, that irascible and invincible old man, Admiral Lord Fisher, had just taken over as First Sea Lord, a position he had previously held from 1904 to 1910. His reaction to the news was in keeping with his doctrine: destroy opposition with overwhelming force wherever it presents itself. Von Spee was to be hunted, found and annihilated, and the necessary deployment had to be carried out with energy and dispatch.

Fisher at once sent orders to Sir John Jellicoe, Commander-in-Chief of the Grand Fleet, to release the *Invincible* and *Inflexible*, 'urgently needed for foreign service'. These sister ships had a displacement of 17,250 tons, an unprecedented speed of twenty-seven knots, and an armament of eight 12-inch and sixteen 4-inch guns. Their fighting strength alone would make the destruction of Von Spee's squadron inevitable if they encountered him. The German squadron was known to consist of two big armoured cruisers, the sister ships *Scharnhorst* and *Gneisenau*, each armed with eight 8-inch guns and six 6-inch, with a maximum speed of twenty-three knots, and the three light cruisers *Leipzig*, *Nürnberg* and *Dresden*.

The *Invincible* and *Inflexible* arrived at Devonport for some dockyard attention on 8 November 1914 and sailed again three days later. The command of them and of the whole operation had been given to Vice-Admiral Sir Frederick Doveton Sturdee, recently Chief of Staff at the Admiralty. His powers were extensive, including command of the ships of any other admiral whose area he entered. The *Invincible* and *Inflexible* refuelled at the Cape Verde Islands on 19 November; by the twenty-sixth they were off the coast of Brazil, where they were joined by Rear-Admiral Stoddart's cruiser squadron which had been operating north of Montevideo, and by some colliers.

Stoddart's flagship was the armoured cruiser *Carnarvon*, armed with four 7.5-inch guns and six 6-inch, and his other ships were the two smaller armoured cruisers *Kent* and *Cornwall*, and the two light cruisers *Bristol* and *Glasgow*. The latter was the one warship to have escaped from the massacre at Coronel; after reaching the Falkland Islands, her commander, Captain Luce, had received orders to join Rear-Admiral Stoddart's squadron.

Sturdee certainly had the ships to annihilate Von Spee's squadron, but first the enemy had to be found. He might be crossing Sturdee's front on his way to South Africa, to assist the Boer rebellion. It had been crushed by now, but Von Spee might not know that. Or had he even come round the Horn? Sturdee had received information from Valparaiso that the *Leipzig* and another German cruiser had put in there on 13 November and left the next day.

BELOW Sir John Jellicoe, Commander-in-Chief of the Grand Fleet.

ABOVE The armoured cruiser
Scharnhorst after the battle of
Coronel, 1 November 1914.

The two British battle-cruisers and five cruisers moved down the South
Atlantic in line abreast, fifty miles from wing to wing. Nothing was seen of the
enemy, and on 7 December they reached the Falklands and began coaling at
once. Time was of the essence and Sturdee intended to put to sea again on the
ninth. At about 08.00 on the eighth, when both battle-cruisers were fully
engaged in coaling and two light cruisers were repairing boilers, a telephone
message came from a lookout post on the heights above Port Stanley: two
warships were fast approaching from the southwest. They were the
Gneisenau and *Nürnberg*.

Von Spee, too, during the past weeks, would have liked to know the whereabouts and strength of enemy forces. And he had other worries. Almost half
the supply of high-explosive shells carried by his heavy cruisers had been
expended at the Battle of Coronel. Another major action would leave them
practically defenceless. And there was the ever-recurrent need of coal; the
Scharnhorst and *Gneisenau* each burnt two hundred tons a day at cruising

speed. On 2 December Von Spee had rounded the Horn with the intention of attacking the Falklands and destroying the installations. There were unlikely to be more than one or two warships at Port Stanley, thought Von Spee, and he had little doubt that he could dispose of them.

At that date, 2 December, his assessment of the situation was substantially correct. Only the old monitor *Canopus* was at Port Stanley as a guardship, and she had been beached to be used as a stationary fort. If Von Spee had continued on to the Falklands he would have been off Port Stanley two days later – when Sturdee and his battle-cruisers were still three days' steaming away. But soon after Von Spee's squadron had rounded the Horn and was south of Staten Island, the *Leipzig* sighted a three-masted barque striving to make westing. On investigation, she proved to be the Canadian-owned *Drummuir* carrying 2,800 tons of good steam coal. This was manna from heaven, and she was taken into the sheltered waters of the Beagle Channel. The other ships followed and on the morning of the third began coaling.

The manna was to be their ruin. The squadron did not put to sea again

ABOVE Vice-Admiral Sir Frederick Doveton Sturdee.

LEFT The *Gneisenau*, sister ship to the *Scharnhorst*.

LEFT The light cruiser *Nürnberg*.

ABOVE Rear-Admiral A. P. Stoddart.

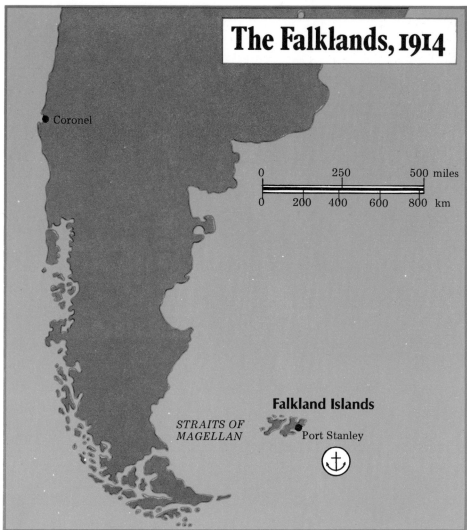

The Falklands, 1914

Coronel

0   250   500 miles

0   200   400   600   800   km

Falkland Islands

STRAITS OF
MAGELLAN   Port Stanley

until 6 December, bound for the Falklands. Soon after dawn on the eighth the *Scharnhorst*, Von Spee's flagship, hoisted the signal to detach, and the *Gneisenau* and *Nürnberg* forged ahead as planned. The *Gneisenau*'s lookouts reported smoke over Port Stanley. This was thought to come from stocks of coal being destroyed before the island was evacuated. But then, as the *Gneisenau* held her course and had a brief look into the harbour, the clear morning light showed a crowd of ships . . . and the tall tripod masts of battle-cruisers. *Gneisenau* made a signal to the flagship, telling what had been seen, and Von Spee replied, 'Do not accept action', shortly followed by, 'Flag to all ships. Get up steam in all boilers.'

The Germans were getting the hell out of it.

Sturdee and his officers were considerably relieved to learn that the *Gneisenau* and *Nürnberg* were hurrying away; the German squadron could have caught the British at a serious disadvantage by attacking them while still in harbour. Perhaps Von Spee had deemed discretion the better part of valour or he was mindful of his ammunition situation.

In record time the British raised steam and proceeded to sea. The *Glasgow* was the first out of harbour, and she worked up to full speed to keep touch with the enemy. The German ships were already hull down on the

LEFT The British light cruiser *Glasgow*.

BELOW The armoured cruiser *Carnarvon*, Rear-Admiral Stoddart's flagship.

ABOVE The pursuit of Von Spee's squadron by W. L. Wylie.

horizon. Soon after 10.00 the two battle-cruisers cleared the harbour, followed shortly by the *Cornwall*. Sturdee ordered the signal 'General chase' to be hoisted.

At 10.48 the *Glasgow* reported that she could see the enemy's mastheads only twelve miles ahead. This was fortunate as the chilly north-westerly breeze was driving the smoke from the battle-cruisers in the direction taken by the Germans. By noon the pursuit was slowly gaining on the enemy. The *Glasgow* was keeping station some three miles ahead of the battle-cruisers; the *Kent* was about two miles astern of them, and the *Carnarvon* and *Cornwall* as much again. Aboard all ships there was an atmosphere of intense excitement; but few of the officers and men had ever heard a shot fired in anger. An exception was the *Glasgow*, whose crew had a frightening knowledge of the realities of a naval battle and were grimly and confidently intent on avenging their comrades lost at Coronel.

The *Leipzig* was seen to be dropping astern of the other four ships, and by 12.50 she was within range of the big guns of the battle-cruisers. She was clearly doomed, and Von Spee made the decision to order his three light cruisers to part company and endeavour to escape, while he tried to hold off the enemy with the *Scharnhorst* and *Gneisenau*.

The two German armoured cruisers swung round to the northeast to engage the British battle-cruisers, while the *Dresden*, *Nürnberg* and *Leipzig* bore away southward, with the *Glasgow*, *Kent* and *Cornwall* in pursuit. And at 13.30 the main battle began, more than sixty miles to the southeast of the Falklands.

The exchange of broadsides – *Invincible* against *Gneisenau*, *Inflexible* against *Scharnhorst* – was at long range at first, 14,500 and then 14,000 yards. The British gunners were groping for their targets and obtained very few hits. So much better was the German gunnery that when the range closed slightly the *Invincible* was hit by a single shell, and Sturdee edged away again. Von Spee endeavoured to slip away behind the smoke; if his luck changed, he might find a rain-squall or a bank of fog in which to disappear.

It was Stoddart, miles astern in the old *Carnarvon*, who saw the Germans

110

turn away, and he made a signal by wireless to the flagship. The battle-cruisers swung round and picked up speed for another chase. By 14.45 the range had closed again to 15,000 yards and the British opened fire on the German cruisers once more. Von Spee held to his southerly course until the range came down to 12,500 yards, then his two ships turned nine points to port in succession to accept battle, and their broadsides thundered in concert. But at this shortened range the 12-inch guns of the battle-cruisers were doing deadly work. Soon after 15.00 the *Scharnhorst* was on fire in several places and the *Gneisenau* had a decided list to starboard. Von Spee kept trying to close the range, to bring his secondary armament into action, but he paid heavily for the attempt. The British gunners were becoming more effective, and the *Scharnhorst*'s upper works were a shambles; her third funnel was gone; fires were blazing; and she was lower in the water. Yet her salvoes were still well-grouped and frequent. She plunged onward through a mass of waterspouts, long gashes now showing in her side, through which could be seen the glare of fires between decks. Suddenly she turned to starboard and came staggering towards her powerful opponents. Her guns had fallen silent, probably because ammunition was exhausted or no longer available, and she tried to close for a last desperate attack with torpedoes. At the same time, 15.55, Von Spee signalled to the *Gneisenau*, 'Endeavour to escape if your engines are still intact.'

The *Scharnhorst*'s speed slackened, her list became more acute, and at 16.10 she was lying on her beam ends. A few minutes later she disappeared, her propellers still turning and her flag still flying. When the *Carnarvon* reached the spot there were neither survivors nor wreckage to be seen.

Even before the *Scharnhorst* sank, a shell from the *Inflexible* had smashed one of the *Gneisenau*'s funnels, and with her starboard engine-room flooded she had no chance of obeying Von Spee's injunction to escape. Her captain was faced with a choice of surrender or annihilation. He could not have wasted much thought on the former course, although his ship was in a terrible

LEFT Vice-Admiral Sturdee's flagship, *Invincible*, at full speed.

ABOVE Picking up survivors from the *Gneisenau*, photographed from the *Invincible*. HMS *Inflexible* is in the background.

BELOW A German medal struck to commemorate the gallantry of Admiral von Spee. With him are his sons, Heinrich and Otto, both of whom were killed in action at the Falklands.

state; casualties had been heavy; many guns were out of action; and speed was down to about eight knots. Yet she kept up a running fight for more than an hour against the three enemy ships, and even scored three hits on the *Invincible*. By 17.15 more than half her crew were dead or badly wounded and the ammunition had all been fired. She was virtually stopped and listing heavily. Sturdee ordered 'Cease fire' and waited for her to strike her flag. Instead, her captain gave orders for the ship to be blown up. The British ships picked up 187 survivors, but the captain was not one of them.

It was then about 18.00, and miles away to the south the light cruisers were coming into action. The Germans had had a ten-mile start over the British, and the *Dresden*, the fastest of them all, never was overhauled. The three Germans had kept in sight of one another for three hours, but when their pursuers drew near enough to fire a few tentative shots they had scattered. Then the *Kent* pursued the *Nürnberg*, while the *Cornwall* and *Glasgow* chased after the *Leipzig*.

There was very little hope for the *Leipzig*. She was the slowest of all the six cruisers and was badly in need of a refit. But her captain and crew put up a splendid fight until all her guns were silent and she was on fire fore and aft. The two British cruisers ceased fire, and Captain Luce signalled by Morse to the stricken ship that he was anxious to save life and asked if she would surrender. There was no answer; the *Leipzig*'s flag still flew and she was even

ABOVE The damaged upper deck
of *Kent*; CPO Layton (under hatch
cover) was awarded the DSM for
his conduct at the battle.

then preparing to loose off torpedoes. The *Glasgow* and *Cornwall* closed to
within 3,000 yards but kept away from the bearings of the *Leipzig*'s torpedo-
tubes. At 19.50 both British cruisers reopened fire, reducing the German ship
to a complete shambles. Then two green flares were seen on her deck, and
Luce decided to accept them as a signal of surrender. The *Glasgow* and
Cornwall each lowered two boats as the *Leipzig* heeled over – the captain had
ordered the sea-cocks to be opened and everyone still alive to go overboard.
There were pitifully few survivors: only five officers and thirteen ratings
were picked up alive, the shock of immersion in the icy water having killed the
others who had jumped overboard.

Meanwhile the *Kent* had been slowly but surely reducing the distance
between herself and the fleeing *Nürnberg*. This was at the cost of all the
wardroom furniture and everything else that would burn, including even the
paymaster's desk and the chaplain's lectern, for the *Kent* had not begun
coaling when the enemy appeared off Port Stanley and her bunkers were low
for a long chase at maximum speed. By the time she came within range of the
Nürnberg men were ripping up deck timbers to help feed the furnaces.

The *Kent*'s starboard batteries opened up, and for twenty minutes the
cruisers pounded each other; with the range gradually shortening, the *Kent*'s
heavier broadside and protective armour gave her the advantage. Although
she was hit about forty times and the radio room was wrecked, casualties

ABOVE Some of the damage inflicted on HMS *Kent* by the *Nürnberg*, before the German cruiser went down.

were light; but the *Nürnberg* suffered severely, becoming a blazing, tangled ruin of a ship. Only two of her guns were still in action; then they too fell silent. The *Kent* ceased firing and moved nearer the *Nürnberg*, which lay about three thousand yards away, burning fiercely – a complete wreck without a sign of life or movement except for her colours, which still fluttered at the peak.

After an interval the *Kent* opened fire again. The *Nürnberg*'s colours were then hauled down – or shot down. At all events, the *Kent* lowered boats to search for survivors. The *Nürnberg* was then sinking fast – her sea-cocks had been opened – and as she went down a group of men was seen to be standing on her stern, apparently singing or cheering. One of them was waving a long piece of wood to which was lashed a German ensign.

The *Kent*'s boats searched the area until dark, but only twelve survivors were found, and five of these died from shock and wounds within a few hours.

All Sturdee's ships were back at Port Stanley on the morning of 10 December. The defeat at Coronel had been more than avenged, and the Germans had not even been able to sell their lives dearly. Damage to the British ships was inconsiderable except for the *Kent*, which had gone in closer than the others to finish off her opponent. Total casualties were ten killed and fifteen wounded. The Germans had lost more than two thousand of their most experienced and courageous naval men. The only German squadron at large on the oceans of the world had been virtually destroyed in a single day.

But Admiral Fisher was not satisfied. The *Dresden* had escaped. Who knew what damage she could cause to British merchant shipping in the South Atlantic? She was eventually found by the *Glasgow* and *Kent* skulking in the Juan Fernandez islands. 'After five minutes' fighting, the *Dresden* hauled down her colours and displayed the white flag,' said the Admiralty announcement of her capture on 14 March 1915.

13 A Classic Naval Battle

The Drama of the Graf Spee, *1939*

The British Admiralty first became aware of the presence of a German surface raider in the South Atlantic on 1 October 1939, when a message was received from Pernambuco saying that the Booth Line steamer *Clement* had been sunk the previous day. During the next two months the raider sank six more British merchantmen over a wide area of ocean, and the Admiralty had deployed eight hunting groups to seek out and destroy the *Admiral Scheer*, as the raider was thought to be.

Actually she was the pocket-battleship *Admiral Graf Spee*, which had sailed from Germany before war was declared and had skulked in areas far from the shipping routes until receiving the signal to proceed on her raiding mission. The *Graf Spee* was one of the three 10,000-ton warships that Germany had been allowed to build under the terms of the Versailles Treaty, and the technicians and shipbuilders had achieved a real *tour de force* with her. She had six 11-inch guns, whereas no 10,000-ton cruiser of any other Power had guns larger than 8-inch; her eight diesel engines gave her a range of action of 20,000 miles at a cruising speed of eighteen knots.

The *Graf Spee*'s complement of nearly 1,200 included a special staff of cypher experts able to break practically any code, and a group of mercantile marine officers, all good English-speakers, who were thoroughly familiar with the trade routes where the *Graf Spee* would operate. Her commander, Kapitän zur See Hans Langsdorff, was a man of exceptional ability and the highest character. He was only forty-two, but had served in the Navy for twenty-seven years and had a wide and varied experience in both sea-going and staff appointments. A cultured man, speaking French and English, he was an officer and gentleman of the old régime and perhaps not the best choice for a command in which absolute ruthlessness was necessary when the crunch came. Captain Harris of the *Clement*, who was held prisoner on board the raider for a time, said later that Langsdorff impressed him as 'a fine sailor of the best type, who had a hearty distaste for the predatory activities he was called upon to perform'. This insight into Langsdorff's character provides a clue to the mysterious circumstances surrounding the *Graf Spee*'s ultimate fate.

The raider had remained most elusive for two months. Then, on 2 December, when north-east of Tristan da Cunha, Langsdorff had his greatest success when he sank the 10,000-ton *Doric Star*, homeward bound with a full cargo of New Zealand meat and butter. But she was also the initial cause of his undoing. Contrary to his usual practice of getting as near as possible before revealing his hostile intent, warning shots were fired at the *Doric Star* at extreme range; and this enabled her to send out a 'shelled by raider' distress signal repeatedly, which was picked up and relayed to a shore station.

At dawn next day another merchantman with food for Britain, the 8,000-ton *Tairoa*, was captured and sunk. She too sent out an 'RRR' call,

The route of the Graf Spee, 1939

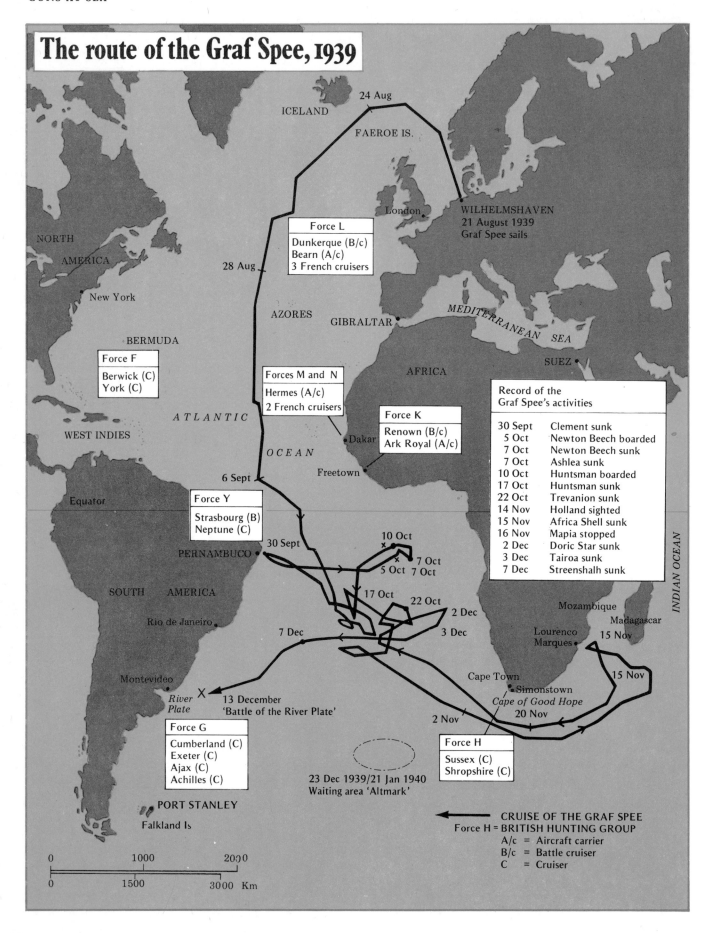

24 Aug

ICELAND

FAEROE IS.

London

WILHELMSHAVEN
21 August 1939
Graf Spee sails

NORTH
AMERICA

28 Aug

New York

Force L

Dunkerque (B/c)
Bearn (A/c)
3 French cruisers

AZORES

GIBRALTAR

MEDITERRANEAN SEA

SUEZ

BERMUDA

Force F

Berwick (C)
York (C)

AFRICA

ATLANTIC

Forces M and N

Hermes (A/c)
2 French cruisers

Force K

Renown (B/c)
Ark Royal (A/c)

WEST INDIES

OCEAN

Dakar

Freetown

**Record of the
Graf Spee's activities**

30 Sept	Clement sunk
5 Oct	Newton Beech boarded
7 Oct	Newton Beech sunk
7 Oct	Ashlea sunk
10 Oct	Huntsman boarded
17 Oct	Huntsman sunk
22 Oct	Trevanion sunk
14 Nov	Holland sighted
15 Nov	Africa Shell sunk
16 Nov	Mapia stopped
2 Dec	Doric Star sunk
3 Dec	Tairoa sunk
7 Dec	Streenshalh sunk

Equator

6 Sept

Force Y

Strasbourg (B)
Neptune (C)

10 Oct

PERNAMBUCO

30 Sept

7 Oct

5 Oct 7 Oct

INDIAN OCEAN

SOUTH   AMERICA

17 Oct

22 Oct

2 Dec

Mozambique

Rio de Janeiro

7 Dec

3 Dec

Madagascar

15 Nov

Lourenco
Marques

15 Nov

Montevideo

Cape Town

Simonstown

Cape of Good Hope

20 Nov

*River
Plate* X

13 December
'Battle of the River Plate'

2 Nov

Force G

Cumberland (C)
Exeter (C)
Ajax (C)
Achilles (C)

23 Dec 1939/21 Jan 1940
Waiting area 'Altmark'

Force H

Sussex (C)
Shropshire (C)

PORT STANLEY

Falkland Is

⟵ CRUISE OF THE GRAF SPEE
Force H = BRITISH HUNTING GROUP
A/c = Aircraft carrier
B/c = Battle cruiser
C = Cruiser

0   1000   2000
0   1500   3000 Km

giving latitude and longitude. This was done while shells from the raider were bursting on the bridge, and stopped only when the wireless-cabin was hit. Five of the *Tairoa*'s crew were wounded by the shelling. They were the first casualties caused by the *Graf Spee*, and Langsdorff was much concerned about them. When Captain Starr of the *Tairoa* arrived on board the raider, Langsdorff sent for him and apologized for firing on a merchant ship, excusing himself by the fact that Starr had failed to obey his signal not to use wireless.

Meanwhile, on the other side of the South Atlantic, Commodore Harwood, commanding one of the hunting forces, had received a vital signal telling him of the two 'RRR' calls. When the two positions were plotted the line showing the direction being taken by the raider pointed towards the River Plate area. Harwood anticipated that the enemy's next objective would be the valuable flow of shipping off that coast, and that at a cruising speed of fifteen knots – the normal, most economical speed of capital ships at the time – the pocket-battleship was likely to be in the River Plate area by the afternoon of 12 December. He therefore proceeded to concentrate his immediately available force – the cruisers *Exeter*, *Ajax* and *Achilles* – in that area.

At dawn on 13 December, a clear dawn with a warm breeze and a calm sea, the three British cruisers were in line ahead, the *Ajax* leading and wearing the Commodore's pendant. At 06.14 the *Exeter* swung out of line to investigate smoke on the horizon – very likely a British or neutral merchantman, as had happened so frequently in past weeks. Two minutes later the *Exeter* flashed the signal, 'I think it is a pocket-battleship'. Action stations were sounded. At 06.18 the enemy opened fire, one 11-inch turret at the *Exeter* and the other at *Ajax*.

The three British warships had been correctly identified aboard the *Graf Spee*. Langsdorff knew they were faster than himself and that he could never have shaken them off; one or the other would have shadowed him until a 'big brother', the battle-cruiser *Renown* or the carrier *Ark Royal*, reached him. So he opened fire before the enemy could get up speed and escape beyond his range. The *Graf Spee*'s chances were good. With her armour and six 11-inch guns she need have nothing to fear from the 8-inch cruiser *Exeter* and the two 6-inch cruisers. Langsdorff had only to keep beyond their range and he could deal with them one after the other.

Harwood's tactical skill in attacking from widely different bearings caused

ABOVE The *Graf Spee* after action with HMS *Exeter*.

the enemy to divide his fire. The pair of light cruisers sped ahead on a slowly closing course, while the *Exeter* turned to a reverse course and closed in more rapidly. The *Graf Spee*'s gunners had to choose between three objectives, while the British could concentrate on the one. The raider's fire was therefore uncertain at first, but after a few minutes all the 11-inch guns were turned on the *Exeter*, which was attacking from the southeast. At 06.24 two direct hits destroyed the *Exeter*'s bridge and one turret and wrecked the steering communications. Further hits put her foremost turrets out of action; but Captain Bell and his men battled on with her one remaining turret, a chain of messengers being formed from the after-conning position.

Meanwhile the *Ajax* and *Achilles* had pressed their attack from the north and gradually closed the range to 8,000 yards. Then the *Graf Spee* brought her main armament to bear on the *Ajax*, while varying her 6-inch guns from her to the *Achilles*. After an hour's fighting, with the *Graf Spee* on a westerly course, the *Ajax*'s after-turrets were knocked out by an 11-inch shell. The pocket-battleship then neglected the *Exeter* and drew nearer the *Achilles* and *Ajax*; the latter fired her torpedoes, but the *Graf Spee* easily evaded them. At 07.38 the range was down to 7,000 yards, the cruisers' ammunition was getting short and the battle had become hopelessly one-sided; Commodore Harwood therefore decided to break off the day battle and re-engage when night came. But when he turned away to the east under cover of smoke the *Graf Spee* did not attempt to follow. Instead she steamed at high speed for the River Plate, and the two light cruisers took up the chase; whenever they drew too near, the *Graf Spee* drove them off with her 11-inch guns. The *Exeter* had been ordered back to the Falklands for badly needed

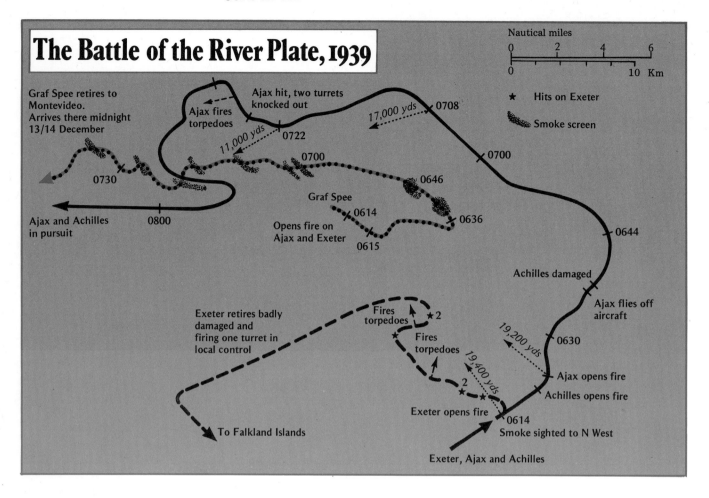

The Battle of the River Plate, 1939

Nautical miles

★ Hits on Exeter

Smoke screen

Graf Spee retires to
Montevideo.
Arrives there midnight
13/14 December

Ajax hit, two turrets
knocked out

Ajax fires
torpedoes

0708

17,000 yds

11,000 yds

0722

0700

0700

0646

0644

0730

0800

Ajax and Achilles
in pursuit

Graf Spee

0614

Opens fire on
Ajax and Exeter

0615

0636

Achilles damaged

Ajax flies off
aircraft

Exeter retires badly
damaged and
firing one turret in
local control

Fires
torpedoes

★ 2

★

Fires
torpedoes

19,200 yds

0630

19,400 yds

2

★

Ajax opens fire

Achilles opens fire

Exeter opens fire

To Falkland Islands

0614

Smoke sighted to N West

Exeter, Ajax and Achilles

repairs; she had fifty-three crew dead and many more seriously wounded.

As *Ajax*'s aerials were down Harwood ordered the *Achilles* to broadcast the *Graf Spee*'s position, course and speed to all British merchant ships. At 09.46 he ordered the 8-inch cruiser *Cumberland*, then at the Falklands, to close the Plate at full speed.

The *Graf Spee* had been hit twenty times, mainly by 6-inch shells. Many of the hits were insignificant. The effective hits, however, had reduced parts of the upper works to a shambles, killing thirty-six men and wounding fifty-eight – including Captain Langsdorff, who was twice nicked by splinters and once knocked out briefly by blast. The galleys were wrecked; many secondary guns were out of action because of ammunition-hoist damage; a 6-inch gun was disabled; much other equipment was damaged; and there were many holes in the deck and sides, including a six-foot-square hole near the waterline.

Her captain had crucial decisions to make. His first inspection convinced him that his ship was not seaworthy enough to attempt a breakthrough to Germany. From that point on, his thoughts and actions appear to have been concerned almost exclusively with his ship and crew; he failed to analyse his tactical and strategic situations. Langsdorff turned his ship towards Montevideo, rejecting Buenos Aires further up the estuary and on the opposite, Argentinian shore (though Argentine was pro-German and Uruguay was not), because the mud in the shallow channel of the Plate beyond Montevideo might clog the water ducts that cooled the engines. It has since been suggested by some of his officers that the temporary concussion he suffered had affected his judgement. His decision to go into Montevideo for repairs was taken without consultation with his senior officers, and was not to their liking.

Harwood, however, while still two hundred miles from the Plate estuary, had to consider the possibility that the *Graf Spee* would turn out to sea. As the gunnery officer of the *Achilles*, Lieutenant Washbourn (later Rear-Admiral and Chief of Staff in New Zealand), wrote to a friend after the action:

We shadowed for the rest of the day, full of speculation as to her intentions . . . Now we refer to this phase of the operations proudly and confidently as the Chase. That was not our attitude at the time. It was unimaginable that this fine ship, with at least one 11-inch turret and one 6-inch in action, and almost her full speed, should be belting from one and a half small 6-inch cruisers both almost out of ammunition. . . .

A diplomatic struggle began in Montevideo very soon after the *Graf Spee* dropped anchor there at midnight. As Uruguay was neutral, under the Hague Convention a belligerent warship could remain only twenty-four hours or long enough to make her seaworthy, otherwise she would be interned. Langsdorff and the German Minister asked for a fortnight's stay to repair

BELOW The *Graf Spee* in flames, scuttled outside the harbour at Montevideo.

RIGHT The *Graf Spee*.

damage – long enough, perhaps, for U-boats to reach the scene and assist the *Graf Spee*. The Uruguayan authorities granted a stay of seventy-two hours. The British, too, had their problems. So far as was known, the *Graf Spee* had not suffered any major damage, and she might still be powerful enough to force a way past the *Ajax* and *Achilles* which were patrolling the hundred-mile-wide Plate estuary. It was necessary to gain time until the arrival of reinforcements.

The British Minister pressed for the internment of the *Graf Spee*. At the same time, in response to Harwood's urgent request, he arranged for the sailing of British merchant ships to delay the raider leaving harbour. The Hague Convention also stipulates that a belligerent warship cannot leave a neutral port until twenty-four hours after the departure of a merchant ship flying the flag of an enemy country. There were six British merchantmen at Montevideo. The *Ashworth* sailed on the evening of 15 December.

The diplomatic struggle continued for another forty-eight hours, during which time the Allied reinforcements drew nearer; though the only ship that actually joined Harwood (now knighted and promoted Rear-Admiral) was the *Cumberland*, which made the dash to the Plate in record time, holding a speed of more than thirty knots for thirty-four hours. But by various propaganda means and intelligence methods Langsdorff and his officers were led to believe that enemy capital ships had arrived off the estuary, and therefore the choice was between interning or scuttling the *Graf Spee*. Langsdorff regarded his chances of breaking past the blockade as minimal, for he would have to keep to the dredged channel and be able to fire only the front turret until out at sea.

On the morning of 16 December Langsdorff addressed his crew and told them he would not sacrifice their lives in a 'death or glory' attempt. Repair work was still going on feverishly; the time limit given to the *Graf Spee* would be up at 20.00 on 17 December. At 18.00 on the sixteenth another British merchantman sailed from Montevideo, thereby severely reducing Langsdorff's freedom of action. Harwood now knew that he would have to come out during the two evening hours on the seventeenth.

In the late afternoon a crowd of 200,000 gathered to watch the *Graf Spee* go out. The three British cruisers closed Montevideo at the time she was due to leave, their guns loaded and their crews at action stations listening – as all the world was listening – to the American broadcasters giving running commentaries from Montevideo breakwater. At 18.15 the *Graf Spee* left harbour with battle ensigns flying, followed by a German merchantman, the *Tacoma*. When the pocket-battleship turned out of the channel to the westward instead of seaward, the crowds were amazed. The crew transferred to the *Tacoma* and some Argentinian tugs; then came a double explosion and the powerful warship suddenly blew up, a mass of flames engulfing her.

Langsdorff had blown up his ship instead of scuttling her because he feared that she might not sink in the shallow waters of the estuary, in which case it was possible that she would fall into the hands of the enemy. Langsdorff took his crew to Buenos Aires, to be interned. He had wanted to set off the explosions himself and go down with his ship, but his officers had dissuaded him. The following night, having seen to the welfare of the ship's company, he shot himself. His flag-lieutenant found him next morning in his hotel room dressed in full uniform and stretched out on the flag of the *Graf Spee*. In one of the letters he left behind he had written: 'A captain with a sense of honour cannot separate his own fate from that of his ship . . . I am happy to pay with my life to prevent any possible reflection on the honour of the flag. . . .'

14 A Very Close-run Thing

Sinking the Bismarck, *1941*

Toward the end of May 1941 the German battleship *Bismarck*, then the most powerful warship afloat, and the heavy cruiser *Prinz Eugen* broke out into the Atlantic. Their presence was a fearful threat to the convoys that were keeping Britain alive. The Admiralty took all possible steps to find and destroy the two raiders, especially the *Bismarck*, but for several days the issue was in doubt.

The *Bismarck* was a brand-new ship, having completed her trials only two months before sailing. She was a sixth of a mile long and displaced 42,000 tons. Her main armament was eight 15-inch guns; she carried six spotter planes, and had a complement of two thousand. The captain was forty-five-year-old Ernst Lindemann, a gunnery specialist; his admiral commanding the squadron was Günther Lütjens, not long returned from a successful raid into the Atlantic with the battle-cruisers *Scharnhorst* and *Gneisenau*, during which he had sunk 116,000 tons of Allied shipping.

The *Bismarck* and the 8-inch cruiser *Prinz Eugen* had sailed from the Baltic in great secrecy during the night of 18 May. But before they even reached the North Sea their presence at sea had been twice reported to the British through Intelligence channels, the information originating first from a Swedish cruiser and then the Norwegian underground. On 21 May a reconnaissance plane of Coastal Command had spotted the two German ships in a fjord near Bergen and had sped back to Scotland with its photographs. A bombing attack was mounted that night, but thick weather had prevented all but two of the eighteen bombers from finding the target area, and those two had dropped their bombs blind.

The weather had continued to favour the Germans. Thick mist and rain covered the North Sea from the Shetlands to the Norwegian coast. Coastal Command cancelled all reconnaissance flights to Norway until further notice. At Scapa Flow the Commander-in-Chief, Admiral Tovey, had brought the fleet to short notice for steam and was waiting anxiously for news. He had made his dispositions. Two 8-inch cruisers, the *Norfolk* and *Suffolk*, were patrolling the Denmark Strait between Greenland and Iceland; two cruisers and five armed trawlers were in the Iceland–Faeroes passage; and on the night of the twenty-first Tovey had ordered the old battle-cruiser *Hood* and the new battleship *Prince of Wales* and a destroyer escort to leave Scapa and take up a position south-west of Iceland, where they could cover both passages into the Atlantic.

Late on 22 May, with the weather as thick as ever, a naval reconnaissance aircraft from Scapa had succeeded in reaching the Norwegian coast and reported that the fjords in the Bergen area were empty of enemy warships. A few hours later Admiral Tovey had sailed from Scapa with the battleship *King George V*, the aircraft-carrier *Victorious* and a cruiser and destroyer escort. On the morning of the twenty-third they were joined by the battle-cruiser *Repulse*, ordered up from the Clyde, and Tovey took his force toward

ABOVE Admiral Günther Lütjens, commander of the German squadron.

OVERLEAF The *Bismarck*, the most powerful warship of its time, photographed in Norwegian waters from the cruiser *Prinz Eugen*, immediately before their Atlantic sortie.

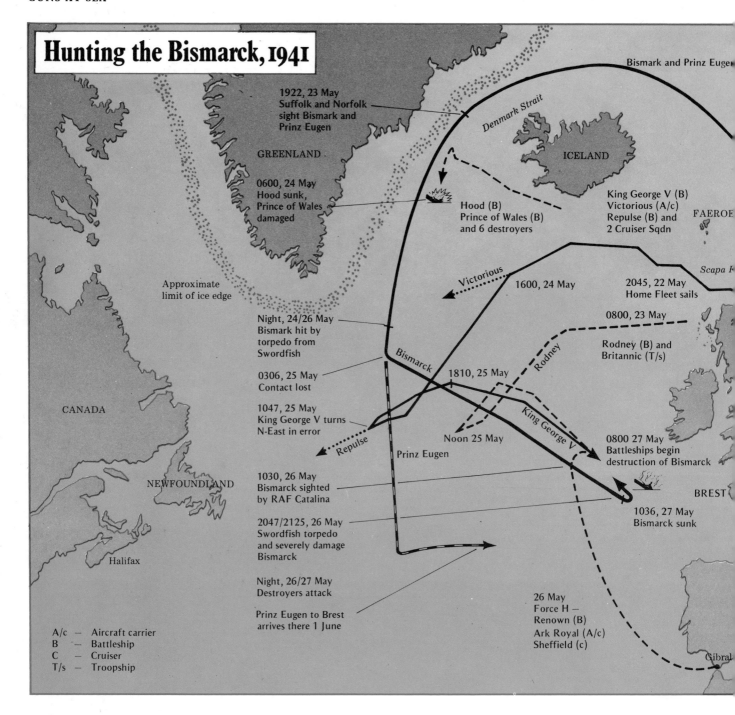

Hunting the Bismarck, 1941

1922, 23 May
Suffolk and Norfolk
sight Bismarck and
Prinz Eugen

0600, 24 May
Hood sunk,
Prince of Wales
damaged

GREENLAND

ICELAND

Bismarck and Prinz Euger

Denmark Strait

Hood (B)
Prince of Wales (B)
and 6 destroyers

King George V (B)
Victorious (A/c)
Repulse (B) and
2 Cruiser Sqdn

FAEROE

Scapa F

Approximate
limit of ice edge

Victorious

1600, 24 May

2045, 22 May
Home Fleet sails

0800, 23 May

Rodney (B) and
Britannic (T/s)

Night, 24/26 May
Bismarck hit by
torpedo from
Swordfish

0306, 25 May
Contact lost

1047, 25 May
King George V turns
N-East in error

Bismarck

1810, 25 May

Rodney

Noon 25 May

King George V

0800 27 May
Battleships begin
destruction of Bismarck

Repulse

Prinz Eugen

BREST

1030, 26 May
Bismarck sighted
by RAF Catalina

1036, 27 May
Bismarck sunk

2047/2125, 26 May
Swordfish torpedo
and severely damage
Bismarck

Night, 26/27 May
Destroyers attack

26 May
Force H —
Renown (B)
Ark Royal (A/c)
Sheffield (c)

CANADA

NEWFOUNDLAND

Halifax

Prinz Eugen to Brest
arrives there 1 June

A/c — Aircraft carrier
B — Battleship
C — Cruiser
T/s — Troopship

Gibral

Iceland in the track of the *Hood* and *Prince of Wales*.

Two days had then passed since the *Bismarck* and her consort had last been sighted; in that time they could have reached the Atlantic unseen. On the other hand, they might still be in Norwegian waters. Most of the twenty-third went by without any news of the German raiders. Then, at about 20.00 came the first of a stream of radio reports of the enemy's position, course and speed. The *Norfolk* and *Suffolk* had sighted the *Bismarck* and *Prinz Eugen* in the mists and snow flurries of the Denmark Strait and were keeping touch a dozen miles astern, chiefly by radar. Tovey's force was then six hundred miles away, the *Hood* and *Prince of Wales* only three hundred and steering a converging course. Vice-Admiral L. Holland, flying his flag in the *Hood*,

TOP RIGHT A coastal command reconnaissance photograph showing *Prinz Eugen* in Hjeete Fjord ready to commence the raiding voyage with *Bismarck* in the Atlantic.

RIGHT Vice-Admiral Tovey and the captain on the quarter-deck of HMS *Prince of Wales*.

SWEDEN

NORWAY

Bergen

ETLAND IS
KNEY IS

Gdynia
18 May 1941
Bismarck and
Prinz Eugen sail

EAT
TAIN

ABOVE The German heavy cruiser *Prinz Eugen*.

signalled his squadron to increase speed. Presently they went to action stations.

At 05.00 on 24 May the opposing forces were within twenty miles of one another. A few minutes later the Germans, much to their surprise, sighted the two British warships and at first took them for cruisers. German Intelligence believed the British capital ships still at Scapa. Dawn was breaking as action was joined at a range of thirteen miles. When the 15-inch guns of the British spoke with their terrible roar, the Germans knew they were not facing cruisers. Lütjens's orders were to avoid action with enemy warships; his task was to reach the Atlantic undamaged and destroy merchant shipping. But now he had no choice.

Vice-Admiral Holland had the advantage in heavy guns, eighteen against eight. But he had handicapped himself by approaching at an angle which enabled only ten of those guns to bear on the enemy. However, there was a reason for this: the *Hood*'s vulnerable upper deck would be exposed to the enemy's long-range fire for the minimum time. There were other disadvantages too. The *Prince of Wales* was fresh from the builder's yard; both ship and crew were raw and untested. And Holland had failed to order the *Norfolk* and *Suffolk* to close up and worry the *Bismarck* from the rear.

The British fire was divided between the *Bismarck* and *Prinz Eugen*, while their fire was concentrated on the *Hood*. Only six minutes after action had been joined a 15-inch shell from *Bismarck*'s broadside plunged like a rocket into the *Hood*'s deck, pierced the steel that should have been strengthened but never was, and exploded in the magazine. She blew up, and all but three of her complement of more than fourteen hundred men were killed.

Now the German ships concentrated their fire on the *Prince of Wales*, and after another twelve minutes of battle she had been hit seven times, including three below the waterline. Her commander, Captain John Leach, made smoke and turned away. But the *Bismarck* had not come through the short action unscathed. She had suffered three hits; one of the shells had penetrated two oil tanks and another had put a boiler-room out of action. So serious was the damage that Lütjens decided he could not carry on with his assignment until dockyard repairs had been effected, and that his best course was to make for a French Atlantic port.

He continued on a southerly course all that day, the twenty-fourth, still tailed by the *Suffolk* and *Norfolk*, who had been joined by the damaged *Prince of Wales*. Meanwhile Tovey was approaching from the east with the *King George V* and *Repulse*, and he expected to bring the Germans to battle early on the twenty-fifth. In the hope of slowing them down and making action more certain, at 15.00 on the twenty-fourth he detached the carrier *Victorious* and her cruiser escort to launch an attack on the *Bismarck* with her Swordfish torpedo-planes. It was past 22.00 before the *Victorious* got within extreme striking range, one hundred miles, for her obsolete bi-planes. Nine of them were flown off, each with a crew of three and with one torpedo slung below the belly. Most of the airmen had never flown on operations at sea before. They found their target – the *Bismarck*, alone, for the *Prinz Eugen*

BELOW The *Bismarck* in action against HMS *Hood* in the early hours of 24 May.

had earlier succeeded in slipping away undetected by the pursuers, obeying Lütjen's orders to act independently – and the airmen gallantly pressed home their attack, scoring one hit amidships. Miraculously, not one of the planes was shot down or even badly damaged; and all returned safely to the *Victorious* during the night.

The one hit had caused very little damage but the *Bismarck*'s twisting and turning to avoid other torpedoes had aggravated the earlier damage, and speed had to be reduced to twenty knots. Moreover, the fuel situation was becoming critical, and the air attack meant that an enemy carrier was within a hundred miles; other planes would be back in the morning for certain. It had become imperative to shake off the ships which had been shadowing the *Bismarck* for more than thirty hours. Lindemann had tried several times already, but now he was successful. At 05.00 on the twenty-fifth Tovey received a signal from the *Suffolk*: 'Have lost contact with enemy.'

The *Victorious* flew off a reconnaissance patrol of seven Swordfish at 07.30 but they failed to sight the *Bismarck*. The Admiralty ordered a number of ships to break off from patrol or convoy escort and to steer towards the *Bismarck*'s presumed course. The nearest to the area were the cruisers *London* and *Edinburgh*, coming up from the Azores, and the old battleship *Rodney* with three destroyers, coming down from the north. Further away, coming from Gibraltar, were the carrier *Ark Royal*, the old battle-cruiser *Renown* and the 6-inch cruiser *Sheffield*. At Coastal Command patrols were sent to cover the *Bismarck*'s most likely tracks to France and to the Faeroes, for she may have turned north-east to get back to Norway. But as night fell on the twenty-fifth there was still no news of the *Bismarck*.

Most of the ships with Tovey were now short of fuel; the *Victorious*, *Suffolk* and *Prince of Wales* had to return to base. The *King George V* had reduced speed to economize on fuel. The *Bismarck*, all unbeknown to her enemies, had only enough fuel left to reach Brest at a cruising speed of twenty knots. Dawn on the twenty-sixth showed the Germans a grey, steep sea that was empty of other ships and an overcast sky empty of planes. By the end of the day the *Bismarck* should be within the range of protective air-cover from France. Half the morning passed without any sign of the British, and the Germans' hopes grew stronger. Then, at 10.30, when less than seven hundred miles from Brest, a Catalina appeared in a break in the clouds. The *Bismarck* opened up an intense anti-aircraft fire; the plane took violent evasive action and disappeared into cloud. Half an hour later two Swordfish put in a brief appearance, which meant that another British carrier could not be far away. But afternoon came and gave way to evening and there were still no attacks. Morale rose among the *Bismarck*'s crew. Another two hundred miles and they would be almost out of danger.

The co-pilot of the Catalina which had sighted the *Bismarck* and radioed her position was an American, Ensign (later Captain) Leonard B. Smith. Although America had not then joined in the war, he wore the uniform of the us Navy and was flying as a 'special observer'; he was at the controls at the time. The news that the *Bismarck* had been found was tempered by the fact that unless she could be slowed down, neither the *King George V* nor the *Rodney* – the battleships with the fire-power to destroy her – would be able to catch her up. The *King George V* was 135 miles to the north of her reported position, the *Rodney* 125 miles to the northeast. However, ahead of the *Bismarck*, between her and Brest, was the squadron from Gibraltar commanded by Vice-Admiral Sir James Somerville: the *Renown*, *Ark Royal* and

OPPOSITE The 8-inch cruisers *Norfolk* (top) and *Suffolk* (bottom).

RIGHT The battleship
HMS *King George V*.

RIGHT The battleship HMS *Rodney*.

OPPOSITE TOP HMS *Dorsetshire*,
the ship which finally sank
the *Bismarck*.

OPPOSITE BOTTOM The captain and
crew of the *Dorsetshire*, in port
after the action.

Sheffield. The *Renown* was of the same vintage as and even more vulnerable than the *Hood*, and the Admiralty had signalled Somerville that she was not to engage the *Bismarck* unless one or other of the two battleships had already engaged. Everything depended upon the *Ark Royal*'s Swordfish torpedo-planes.

At 13.15 on the twenty-sixth Somerville ordered the *Sheffield* to steer for the *Bismarck*, then forty miles away, and shadow her. An hour-and-a-half later a striking force of fifteen torpedo-planes took off from the *Ark Royal*. Somerville signalled the result of the attack to Tovey with the dismal and laconic words, 'Estimate no hit.' He deemed it not advisable at the time to add that the pilots had mistaken the *Sheffield* for the *Bismarck*; they had been informed too late that the *Bismarck* was being trailed, yet should have recognized the two-stack cruiser from the one-stack enemy battleship.

Fortunately the *Sheffield* had evaded all the torpedoes.

Somerville signalled 'Second striking force will leave *Ark Royal* about 18.30.' Tovey had little reason to think that it would be any more successful than the first, and time was fast running out. He had just informed the Admiralty that unless the *Bismarck* was slowed down by midnight, the *King George V* would have to return to harbour for lack of fuel. The result of the second attack was not unexpected: 'Estimate no hits.' But a few minutes later a signal which arrived from the *Sheffield* was almost beyond belief: 'Enemy's course 340.' The *Bismarck* was steering north-northwest – directly towards the *King George V* and *Rodney*! This was confirmed by a signal from a shadowing Swordfish. What had happened to the *Bismarck*?

The *Ark Royal*'s planes had after all obtained two hits, late in the attack, and one of them had struck right aft and damaged the steering gear compartment. The rudders were jammed, and despite all efforts they remained jammed. And although Captain Lindemann tried every combination of orders to the engine-room, it proved impossible to steer the ship in the desired direction by propellers alone. The *Bismarck* was unmanœuvrable. The fatal hit was a chance in a million.

Before midnight a destroyer flotilla commanded by Captain Vian in the *Cossack*, which had earlier been detached from escorting a troop convoy, came up and made several torpedo attacks on the *Bismarck* during the night. But there was nothing wrong with her armament and she kept the destroyers at a distance. The rough sea and black night were not helpful either, and although the destroyers fired all their torpedoes, they made no hit. But when dawn came the destroyers were on station, maintaining contact with the crippled battleship and reporting her position to Tovey, who had decided to postpone attack until daylight. Vian's flotilla had done their essential job.

All available U-boats were making for the *Bismarck*; squadrons of German bombers were on the way from France, as were three tugs to take the *Bismarck* in tow. They were all too late. At 08.45 on 27 May the *Rodney* and *King George V*, sailing in line abreast and half-a-mile apart, opened fire on the *Bismarck* from twelve miles range. When the range was down to ten miles the *Norfolk*, which had sped through the night to be in at the kill, joined in with her 8-inch guns. And soon after nine the cruiser *Dorsetshire* arrived on the scene from the south. The *Bismarck* was firing salvo after salvo at the *Rodney*, then shifted her fire to the *King George V*, but without scoring a direct hit on either battleship. Then her fire diminished rapidly as shells from the four British ships tore into her. By 10.00 she was a battered burning wreck but her flag was still flying. It remained to finish her off, to sink her. Only one ship, *Dorsetshire*, still had torpedoes. She went in close and fired three; all hit, and the *Bismarck* rolled over and sank stern first, leaving scores of men swimming in the oily water. The *Dorsetshire* picked up eighty of them, a destroyer twenty-four.

The menace to Britain's life-lines was eliminated, but it had been a very close-run thing.

The German bombers which had set out from French bases sank one destroyer, but all other British ships which took part in the sinking of the *Bismarck* returned safely to base. As for the *Prinz Eugen*, she developed serious engine trouble and shaped course for Brest, where she arrived safely on 1 June.

15 The Japs have it all their Own Way

Java Sea, 1942

After Singapore and its garrison surrendered on 12 February 1942, the Japanese invasion convoys swept on to make landings in the Dutch East Indies. In the second half of February the Japanese had troops ashore in eastern Sumatra, southern Borneo, Celebes and Timor. Ports and towns in Java were being subjected to heavy air attacks. The Allied naval forces available to oppose the Japanese drive across the Java Sea were lamentably few compared with the might of the enemy. There were no Allied capital ships in the area; none, in fact, within ten thousand miles. The opposition to the Japanese rested upon a hastily assembled squadron of British, Dutch, Australian and American cruisers of mixed vintage supported by a couple of flotillas of old destroyers. This force, without air cover, without proper communications, faced the powerful resources of the world's third largest navy. The most the Allied ships could hope for was some limited tactical success, some delaying action.

An Allied Command called ABDA (the initials of the four navies concerned) had been set up on 15 January with headquarters in western Java. The Supremo was Field Marshal Sir Archibald Wavell and the Naval Commander was an American, Admiral Thomas Hart. But the Netherlands Government in exile in London wanted their own man, Vice-Admiral C. Helfrich, as commander of the naval forces. He had been born and bred in Java; he and his compatriots were fighting to defend their homeland. Washington agreed to recall Admiral Hart on grounds of ill-health (he was sixty-four but still hale and hearty), and on 16 February Helfrich took over a command which was already stretched to the limit and was in no way unified.

On 25 February air reconnaissance reported three large Japanese convoys and escorts sailing southward to Java. Admiral Helfrich, from ABDA headquarters at Lembang in western Java, proceeded to concentrate the naval units under his command at Sourabaya, the naval base on the northeast coast of Java, to meet this three-pronged menace. On the twenty-sixth a conference of all commanding officers was held ashore, presided over by Helfrich's deputy, Rear-Admiral Karel Doorman. By then, the ABDA Command had crumbled away. Wavell and his American deputy commander had flown out. The overall command of the three Services was left in the hands of the stubborn Dutch.

Doorman told the British, American and Australian officers at the conference of his intention to repel first the invasion convoy heading for eastern Java and then to move to the west to attack the main force making for western Java. It was all very brave but completely unrealistic. He added that there was a possibility of fighter protection, an announcement which prompted a burst of bitter laughter along the table.

Doorman, flying his flag in the Dutch 6-inch cruiser *De Ruyter*, took his

ABOVE The Dutch 6-inch cruiser
De Ruyter, Rear-Admiral Karel
Doorman's flagship.

ships to sea late in the evening of 26 February, soon after the conference ended. He had no aircraft carrier, not even a scout plane aboard any of his cruisers, and Intelligence reports from Helfrich's headquarters were so sparse that he had only a general idea of the whereabouts of the Japanese invasion convoys. He led his squadron north and then east and searched for the enemy throughout that calm, moonlight night. Steaming astern of the *De Ruyter* were four other cruisers, two of them heavy ships carrying 8-inch guns: HMS *Exeter* and USS *Houston*. The *Exeter*, famous for her part in the fight against the *Graf Spee*, had a very experienced crew under the command of Captain Oliver Gordon. The third cruiser was the Australian *Perth*, armed with eight 6-inch guns. The last cruiser in the line was another Dutchman, the 6-inch *Java*. Screening the cruiser line were three British destroyers, the *Electra*, *Encounter* and *Jupiter*, and two antiquated Dutch destroyers; bringing up the rear were four American destroyers built in 1919.

All these ships were battle-scarred from recent skirmishes with the enemy; the most serious damage was to the *Houston*, which had had her after 8-inch gun-turret destroyed by a bomb and so had one-third of her main armament out of action and was unable to fire astern. In all the ships the crews were suffering from the fatigue and strain of much action and weeks of almost continuous time at sea.

Soon after daybreak on 27 February, having had no sight of the enemy, Doorman turned his squadron south to return to Sourabaya. Early in the afternoon the five cruisers and nine destroyers were approaching the swept channel into Sourabaya harbour when Doorman received a signal from Helfrich's headquarters: patrol aircraft had reported a Japanese convoy and escort in a position northwest of Sourabaya and steaming south at about twenty-four knots. Doorman had intended his ships to take in supplies and fuel, then proceed to sea again that night to make another sweep. But Helfrich's orders were to attack at once, so the *De Ruyter* swung round and signalled, 'Follow me. The enemy is ninety miles away.'

The report was only true in part. The Allied squadron, battle ensigns

ABOVE HMS *Exeter*, famous for her fight against the *Graf Spee*.

bravely flying, steamed through the calm sea in line ahead at twenty-five knots. When less than thirty miles from the Java coast, at 16.00, the leading destroyer sighted a cruiser and a number of destroyers; shortly afterwards the *Exeter* sighted another flotilla of destroyers led by a cruiser. They were the close support group of an invasion convoy comprising forty-one transports and supply ships. This group of thirteen destroyers and two light cruisers was inferior, at least on paper, to Doorman's squadron. But the Japanese crews were fresh, their morale was high; and more to the point, they knew that the convoy had distant cover from the two heavy cruisers *Nachi* and *Haguro*, each armed with ten 8-inch guns.

These two cruisers came speeding up and opened fire with their full 8-inch broadsides at the extreme range of 28,000 yards. Their targets were the *Exeter* and *Houston*, which replied with several salvoes; but at that range neither side scored a hit. The urgent need for Doorman was to close the range to enable his superiority in 6-inch gun-power to make itself felt. The Japanese fire was becoming unpleasantly accurate, for the gunnery officers had the great advantage of assistance from three spotting aircraft. Meanwhile the British destroyers had come under attack from the *Jintsu*. This light cruiser carried seven 5.5-inch guns. She led her destroyer flotilla directly towards the *Electra* and at a range of 18,000 yards straddled her with the first two salvoes. The *Electra* and *Jupiter* replied with their 4.7-inch guns when the range had closed to less than 16,000 yards, but even then their

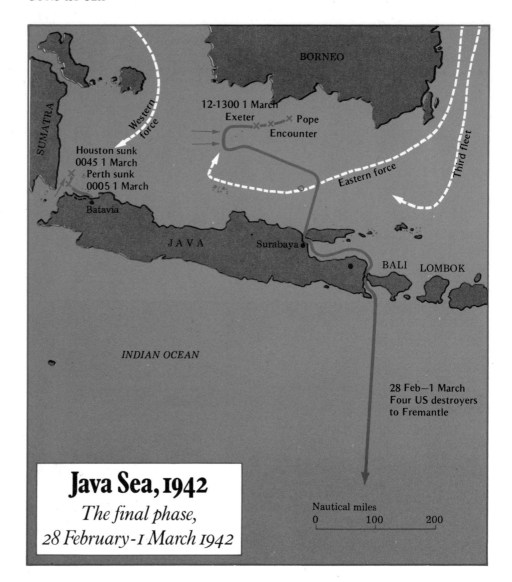

BORNEO

12-1300 1 March
Exeter ×—×—× × Pope
Encounter

Western force

Third fleet

SUMATRA

Houston sunk
0045 1 March
Perth sunk
0005 1 March

Eastern force

Batavia

J A V A   Surabaya

BALI   LOMBOK

INDIAN OCEAN

28 Feb—1 March
Four US destroyers
to Fremantle

Java Sea, 1942
*The final phase,
28 February-1 March 1942*

Nautical miles
0   100   200

salvoes fell far short. The Japanese practice of employing a light cruiser as destroyer flotilla leader was paying off in this battle, as it was to do in future actions in the Pacific.

Doorman was still closing the range, and at 16.35 Admiral Takagi, wearing his flag in the *Nachi*, ordered a torpedo attack on the enemy cruisers. Seven destroyers raced at thirty-five knots to unleash their much-vaunted oxygen-fuelled torpedoes, but not a single one hit. The battle was being carried northward and smudges of smoke on the horizon showed that Doorman was pressing close to his primary objective – the invasion convoy. Takagi, realizing this, signalled his ships to close the enemy. All Doorman's cruisers except the *Perth* had been hit but none of the damage was serious; both heavy cruisers had claimed hits on Japanese ships. Then suddenly, just as another Japanese torpedo attack was delivered, the tide of battle turned drastically against the Allies.

The *Exeter* had been the enemy's main target – at one time all the Japanese cruisers were concentrating their fire upon her – and at 17.07 she was struck by a shell which exploded in a boiler room, killing all ten men in it and putting six boilers out of action. The *Exeter*'s speed dropped alarmingly; Captain Gordon turned his ship to port and hauled out of line, to avoid

LEFT The Japanese light cruiser *Jintsu*.

being struck by the *Houston* astern. The *Kortenaer*, one of the two Dutch destroyers, was hit amidships by a torpedo during this confusion. She broke in two; the stern half soon sank, but the bow remained pointing upwards. Doorman ordered the *Exeter* to return to Sourabaya and detached the Dutch destroyer *Witte de With* to escort her. As the British cruiser began to retire southward, Doorman ordered the three British destroyers to attack with torpedoes.

The sun was beginning to set and the whole battle area was covered with smoke. The three British destroyers were widely separated and had to attack independently, darting into the murk and firing at whatever enemy units they saw, then retiring again to the Allied side of the smoke. The *Electra* found herself under fire from a light cruiser and several destroyers, and furiously engaged them single-handed. She was repeatedly hit and her guns were silenced one by one. When only one gun remained in action and she was settling in the water, her captain gave the order to abandon ship. The *Electra* went down with her flag flying at about 18.00.

The *Exeter* having left the scene, Doorman had only the *Houston*'s six guns to reply to the twenty of the two Japanese 8-inch cruisers. And the *Houston*, which had set out with her ammunition stocks already depleted, was left with only fifty rounds per gun. Fortunately the Japanese admiral was not aware of this, nor of the damaged state of the *Exeter*; otherwise he might well have used his now overwhelming superiority in a more aggressive manner. Instead he decided to break off the action and to give closer protection to the invasion convoy, which was after all his top priority.

Night fell fast. Doorman led his cruisers northeast in an attempt to work round the enemy force and reach the convoy. But he was without any reliable information. When he sent a radio message to Helfrich, 'Enemy retreating west. Where is convoy?' the reply he received was to the effect that his guess was better than any. And so it was, for he was then steaming directly towards the convoy, though it was not yet in sight. But at 19.27 there was a short, sharp engagement with four ships which were sighted to the westward. Doorman had second thoughts: while he was continuing to fight Japanese cruisers and destroyers, the convoy might have turned southward and be making for the coast of Java. So he reversed course and headed for Java to

BELOW The Dutch destroyer *Witte de With*.

try to intercept the convoy. When he was approaching Sourabaya Strait he led round to starboard and kept about four miles from the coast.

The four American destroyers needed to refuel, so put into Sourabaya. Soon afterwards the *Jupiter* struck a mine. She stayed afloat long enough for most of the crew to launch boats and rafts, and they reached the Java coast. Later the *Perth* passed close to a number of men in the water. They were survivors from the *Kortenaer*. Captain Waller of the *Perth* signalled the *Encounter* to stop and pick them up. This she did and then turned back to land them at Sourabaya.

Doorman was thus left without any destroyer support, but he may well have been unaware of this. In any case, the end was near. Doorman turned north, out into the Java Sea again, still doggedly seeking the Japanese convoy. Instead, the two Japanese 8-inch cruisers found him. At about 23.00 the *Nachi* and *Haguro* opened fire at extreme range, then closed to 9,000 yards and launched torpedoes. The *Perth* fired several salvoes and claimed two or three hits. One enemy shell hit the *De Ruyter* on the quarter-deck and she turned away, the other cruisers conforming. When the line was halfway round this turn the *Java* was hit by a torpedo; her after-part blew up, she lost way and came to a stop burning furiously. A few moments later there was a terrific explosion aboard the *De Ruyter* as a torpedo struck her aft; more explosions followed and she settled in the water with several fires burning. The *Perth* just avoided the blazing wreck by the use of full port rudder, while the *Houston* headed out to starboard.

Doorman's verbal orders before sailing from Sourabaya had been that 'any ship disabled must be left to the mercy of the enemy'. Waller, as senior officer of the two remaining ships, took the *Houston* under his command, made a feint to the southeast in breaking off the action, then shaped course

LEFT The Australian cruiser
HMS *Perth*.
BELOW The USS *Houston*.

RIGHT HMS *Exeter* going down.

westward at high speed for the prearranged rendezvous after night action, Tanjong Priok, the port of Batavia. The two cruisers reached there safely at 13.30 next day.

They and the other Allied ships which had survived the battle were ordered to refuel and get clear of the fateful Java Sea; to remain any longer would be suicidal.

At Sourabaya were the *Exeter* and the Dutch destroyer *Witte de With* which had escorted her safely into harbour; also the *Encounter*, the four American destroyers, and a fifth, the *Pope*, which had been undergoing repairs when the squadron had sailed on the night of the twenty-sixth. The commander of the American destroyers received orders from Lembang to escape through the narrow Bali Strait; but he was to leave the *Pope* – which still had all her torpedoes – to escort the *Exeter*. The four American destroyers sailed from Sourabaya late in the afternoon of 28 February, and under cover of darkness passed safely through the Bali Strait into the Indian Ocean.

The *Exeter*, *Encounter* and *Pope* sailed at dusk for the Sunda Strait. The much nearer Bali Strait was considered too shallow for the *Exeter*. (The *Witte de With* needed repairs and was unable to sail with the other three ships; she was later bombed to destruction as she lay alongside the quay.) To reach the Sunda Strait, Captain Gordon had been told to proceed well out into the Java Sea, north from Sourabaya, before turning westward, in order to avoid the warships protecting the Japanese convoys already landing troops on the northern coast of Java.

At Batavia, the *Perth* and *Houston* also received orders to make for the Sunda Strait that same night, 28 February. Their captains, like Gordon, were under no illusions as to their chances. In fact a strong Japanese task force was already guarding the approaches to the Sunda Strait, while also giving cover to another landing in progress. The two Allied cruisers sighted the anchored transports and sank at least four of them by gunfire. It was a last defiant effort. At the entrance to the Sunda Strait the *Perth* and *Houston* were attacked by a dozen cruisers and destroyers, and went down fighting to the last, a little after midnight. A few hundred survivors were made prisoner, and about a third of these died in captivity.

At the time these two gallant cruisers were sunk, the *Exeter* and her two accompanying destroyers were well out in the Java Sea. Gordon altered course to the west at about 04.00 and by the early hours of daylight had covered almost half the distance to the Sunda Strait. Lookouts sighted the top-masts of two warships, and Gordon turned away; he thought he had evaded detection, but the enemy ships had catapulted scouting planes. By mid-morning the little Allied force was ringed around by the *Nachi* and *Haguro*, two other heavy cruisers and a couple of destroyers. The issue was never in doubt. The *Exeter* fought until all her guns were silenced and she was a drifting wreck. Gordon ordered abandon ship, and the survivors went overboard just before the Japanese destroyers sped in and fired torpedoes. The *Exeter* rolled over, dipped her stern and sank. A few minutes later the *Encounter* went down, firing until the end. The USS *Pope* made smoke and headed for a rain squall. She reached it, then another, and her captain began to have hopes of escaping detection and making a dash southward for the Bali or the Lombok Strait. But at 12.30 six dive-bombers came roaring over and repeatedly scored hits on the fleeing destroyer. She still steamed on, spitting fire; not until the bombers had made a dozen runs over her did they bring her to a stop, several compartments flooded and settling aft. The ship was abandoned after demolition charges had been set, and as the boats drew clear she came under heavy fire from Japanese cruisers.

On the afternoon of 1 March 1942 the last Allied warship in the Java Sea, the American *Pope*, sank stern first with her flag still flying.

16 The Beginning of the End

Midway, 1942

ABOVE Admiral Yamamoto, the Japanese commander-in-chief.

One of the most decisive battles of the world was fought near Midway Island in early June 1942. If not the biggest it was certainly the most important battle of the war in the Pacific. It brought to an end the run of Japanese victories, and also showed that henceforth the aircraft-carrier would be a decisive factor in sea warfare. At the Battle of Midway, Japan lost the war in the Pacific and the battleship lost its place as capital ship.

The Japanese Commander-in-Chief, Admiral Yamamoto, was convinced that an invasion of Midway would bring out the US Pacific Fleet, and that his superior strength in carriers would then enable him to gain a decisive victory. At the end of April 1942 Japan had seven large and four small carriers in the Pacific, while all reports showed that the United States had only four. The Japanese plan provided for a powerful carrier striking force which would soften up Midway and the American aircraft on it by bombing and strafing raids. When the island was sufficiently reduced, a strong invasion force would go in to secure it. A diversionary attack would be made on the Aleutian Islands, in the hope of dividing the American naval and air forces. D-Day was fixed for 7 June. The various forces therefore put to sea between 26 and 29 May. Yamamoto commanded the battle fleet, flying his flag in the *Yamato*, a new, 65,000-ton battleship armed with 18-inch guns, the largest and most powerful afloat. Vice-Admiral Nagumo was in command of the carrier force, Kondo of the invasion force, while Hosogaya directed the diversionary attack on the Aleutians.

The Japanese still lacked information on the latest situation of the US Fleet at Hawaii. On the other hand, American Intelligence had broken the Japanese code, and as early as 20 May Admiral Chester Nimitz, Commander-in-Chief of the US Pacific Fleet, knew the exact Japanese order of battle. By 3 June the Pacific Fleet, such as it then was, had taken a waiting position some two hundred miles north-east of Midway, and constant air patrols from the island were being maintained over an arc seven hundred miles out to the west.

Nevertheless the disparity between the two forces about to clash was colossal. The Japanese had eleven battleships, the Americans none. The Japanese had eight aircraft-carriers to the Americans' three; twenty-two cruisers to thirteen; sixty-five destroyers to twenty-eight; twenty-one submarines to nineteen; and seven hundred aircraft to little more than three hundred. At one time it had seemed that Admiral Nimitz would have only two carriers at his disposal, the *Hornet* and *Enterprise*. A third, the *Yorktown*, had been badly damaged in the Battle of the Coral Sea on 8 May and was reported as needing ninety days in dock for repairs. Nimitz appealed to the engineers and ship-repairers, and they performed the first amazing feat in the Midway operation. The damaged *Yorktown* docked at Pearl Harbor on the afternoon of 27 May and was at once taken over by an army of engineers, welders and shipwrights – fourteen hundred craftsmen who

ABOVE Admiral Yamamoto's flagship, *Yamato*, the largest and most powerful battleship afloat at the time.

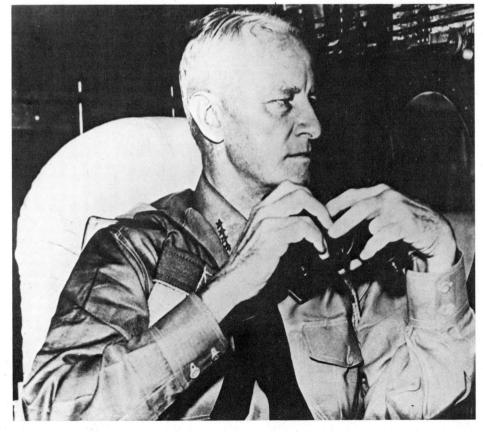

LEFT Admiral Chester Nimitz, the commander-in-chief of the US Pacific fleet.

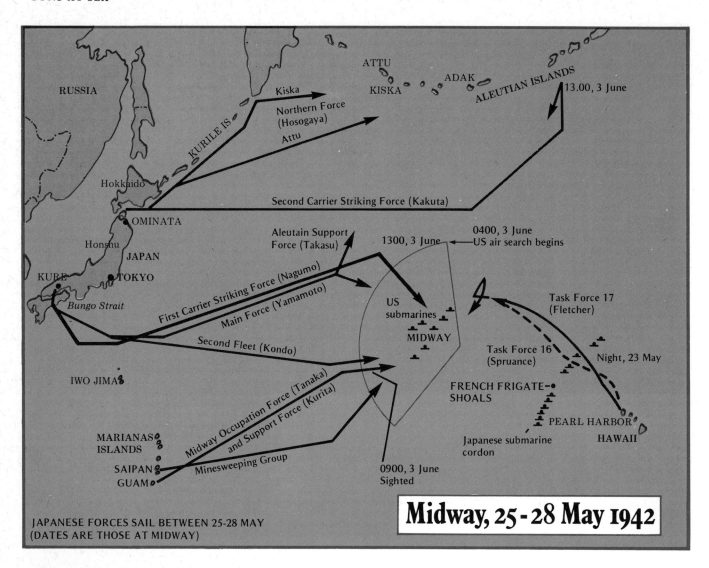

JAPANESE FORCES SAIL BETWEEN 25-28 MAY
(DATES ARE THOSE AT MIDWAY)

Midway, 25-28 May 1942

ABOVE Rear-Admiral Frank
Jack Fletcher.

worked round the clock and got the carrier ready for sea again in forty-eight hours instead of the three months envisaged. The *Yorktown* left dock on 29 May, took on supplies and aircraft, and was away to sea on the thirtieth, wearing the flag of Rear-Admiral Fletcher and making for the position assigned to her north-east of Midway.

The first warning of the Japanese approach was sent at 09.00 on 3 June by the pilot of a Catalina from Midway. Ensign Jack Reid was on patrol some seven hundred miles west of Midway. He had already continued beyond the time when he should have started to return to base, and then sighted what he took to be the main enemy force about thirty miles away. The Catalina started to shadow it, while sending urgent reports. It was in fact the troop transports group and close escort commanded by Rear-Admiral Tanaka. A few hours later the fighting for Midway began when nine Flying Fortresses found Tanaka's convoy 570 miles from the island and made three high-level attacks. They were unsuccessful, though the optimistic aviators reported hits on two battleships and two troop transports. Tanaka had no battleships in his group. But it would not be the last mistake in identification, nor the last unsuccessful bombing attack, in this battle which was destined to continue for three days.

Rear-Admiral Fletcher, waiting with the carriers north-east of Midway, rejected the reports that this was the enemy's main force and, relying on Intelligence reports that the Japanese carriers would approach from the northwest, moved his force southwest during the night to be between Midway and the presumed course of the enemy.

Twelve hundred miles to the north, Hosogaya's invasion convoy had almost reached the position from where aircraft from his two carriers were to fly off to raid Dutch Harbor. Hardly had they disappeared than American aircraft were sighted over the Japanese carriers. So here, too, the enemy was expecting them! The Japanese attack was nevertheless satisfactory. The pilots found the sky clear over Dutch Harbor and caused considerable damage to installations. The Japanese diversion might well have been taken for the main attack if Tanaka's transports had not been sighted heading towards Midway. As it was, Nimitz remained prepared for Nagumo's attack, and air patrols were searching the sea for the Japanese carriers; they were eventually sighted at 05.34 on 4 June by a Catalina pilot belonging to the same squadron as Reid.

Nagumo's carriers had reached their planned position, 240 miles north-west of Midway, an hour before and had flown off the first striking force at 04.45. It consisted of dive-bombers, torpedo-carrying bombers and fighter planes, a total of 108 aircraft. This formation was detected by radar on

ABOVE Vice-Admiral Nagumo, commander of the first carrier striking force at Midway.

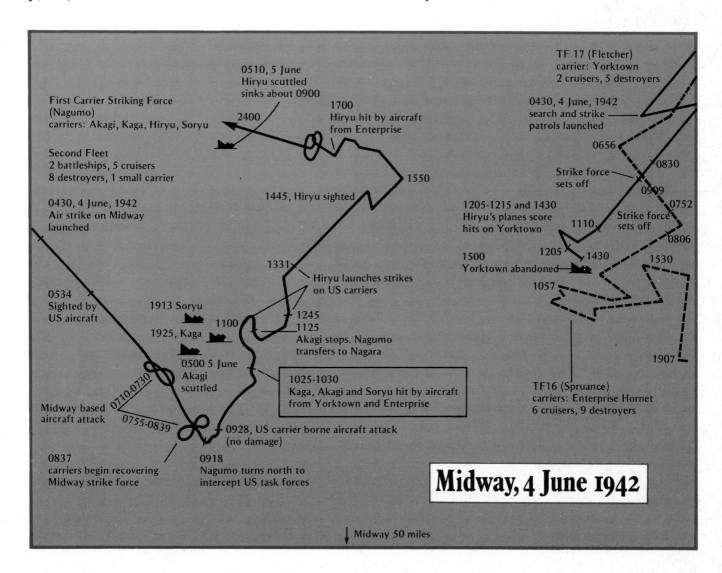

TF 17 (Fletcher)
carrier: Yorktown
2 cruisers, 5 destroyers

0510, 5 June
Hiryu scuttled
sinks about 0900

1700
Hiryu hit by aircraft
from Enterprise

2400

First Carrier Striking Force
(Nagumo)
carriers: Akagi, Kaga, Hiryu, Soryu

Second Fleet
2 battleships, 5 cruisers
8 destroyers, 1 small carrier

0430, 4 June, 1942
Air strike on Midway
launched

0430, 4 June, 1942
search and strike
patrols launched

0656

0830

0909

0752

Strike force
sets off

0806

1550

1445, Hiryu sighted

1205-1215 and 1430
Hiryu's planes score
hits on Yorktown

1110

Strike force
sets off

1331

Hiryu launches strikes
on US carriers

1500
Yorktown abandoned

1205

1430

1530

0534
Sighted by
US aircraft

1913 Soryu

1100

1245
1125

Akagi stops. Nagumo
transfers to Nagara

1057

1907

1925, Kaga

0500 5 June
Akagi
scuttled

1025-1030
Kaga, Akagi and Soryu hit by aircraft
from Yorktown and Enterprise

0710-0730

Midway based
aircraft attack

0755-0839

0928, US carrier borne aircraft attack
(no damage)

TF16 (Spruance)
carriers: Enterprise Hornet
6 cruisers, 9 destroyers

0837
carriers begin recovering
Midway strike force

0918
Nagumo turns north to
intercept US task forces

Midway, 4 June 1942

↓ Midway 50 miles

Midway at 05.53, when still about ninety miles away. By 06.00 every US plane was off the ground. The bombers and Catalinas were ordered to keep well away, while the fighter planes gained altitude; but the latter became so occupied defending themselves against the Zero fighters (thus called by US airmen because the nose of the plane had a circle round it) that the Japanese bombers were hindered only by anti-aircraft fire. Much damage was caused, though less than the Japanese had hoped; the runway could still be used, and the Japanese air commander reported that another attack was needed. The Zeros shot down fifteen of the US fighter planes. All but six of the 108 Japanese aircraft returned to their carriers.

It was during this raid that the Catalina had sighted the Japanese carriers. The first attack on them was made by torpedo-carrying bombers from Midway. They were only ten, without any fighter escort; they went in at low level, were met by a hail of fire from the ships as well as being set on by Zeros; only three of the ten got back to Midway, and not one torpedo had hit. The second attack by a squadron of bombers did no better. Only eight of the sixteen returned to Midway, and six of those were write-offs. Fifteen Flying Fortresses attacked next, at 08.10, each dropping about four tons of bombs from 20,000 feet but without obtaining a single hit. The Fortresses were followed ten minutes later by eleven Vindicators, which had no greater success with their bombs. Two of them were shot down, but all the Fortresses got safely back to Midway.

The day had begun badly for the Americans, but Nagumo then made a faulty decision which gave the Americans a great opportunity. Japanese reconnaissance planes had sighted the US naval force and the reports reached Nagumo at a time when a second strike of planes loaded with bombs was lined up on his carriers' flight-decks; but torpedoes rather than bombs were required for this new target. The first striking force had returned from Midway and its 102 planes were wanting to land on their carriers; some were damaged, all were short of fuel. Should the planes waiting to make an attack be flown off or sent below? Nagumo decided to send them below – and while there the bombs could be replaced by torpedoes. There were hectic scenes on the lower decks of the *Akagi* and *Kaga*, and in their haste the mechanics unfortunately left the bombs lying about instead of stowing them away in their racks there and then.

The last plane landed at 09.18 and Nagumo at once speeded north at thirty knots to reduce the distance between himself and the American force, which he intended to attack at 10.30 with sixty torpedo-carrying aircraft.

Meanwhile Fletcher had made a momentous decision. His original plan was to fly off his first striking force at 09.00, by which time his carriers, heading towards the enemy at twenty-five knots, would have closed seventy-five miles of the distance between the two groups. But reports of the raid on Midway caused him to change his mind. His staff estimated that the Japanese planes returning from Midway would be landing on their carriers at about 09.00. This would be the enemy's weakest moment. So at 07.00 the US carriers swung into the wind to launch their strike while still two hundred miles from the enemy.

But things went wrong. The Japanese had altered course and were not where they should have been. The first planes from the *Enterprise* and *Hornet* reached the estimated enemy position and found the sea empty. Thirty-five of the *Hornet*'s dive-bombers and their fighter cover turned towards Midway, hoping to sight the Japanese on the way. Most of the

bombers had to land on Midway to refuel; all the Wildcat fighters ran out of fuel and had to make forced landings on the sea. The *Hornet*'s fifteen torpedo-carrying planes turned in the opposite direction. Led by Lt-Commander John C. Waldron, they sighted smoke on the horizon and changed course toward it. At 09.25 they went in to attack the Japanese carriers, but without fighter escort. It was a massacre. The Zeros on patrol and the anti-aircraft fire from the ships made short work of the lumbering bombers, all of which pressed home their attack with determination. But no hit was obtained, and of the thirty men in the fifteen planes only one survived; he was rescued from his rubber dinghy by a Catalina the following afternoon.

A few minutes later the fourteen torpedo-carrying aircraft from the *Enterprise* attacked, also without fighter escort. All but four were shot down, and again no damage was caused to the enemy. Then the *Yorktown*'s planes went in; they had fighter cover – six planes which were almost at once destroyed by Zeros. Nevertheless the leader of the squadron, Lt-Commander Massey, bravely pressed home his attack on the *Soryu*. Six aircraft

ABOVE Mitchells taking off from USS *Hornet* by Norman Wilkinson.

151

RIGHT USS *Hornet* in action.

including his own were shot down in flames before they had even fired their torpedoes. The other six succeeded in getting within range, but all missed their target and only three of them returned to their carrier.

It seemed hopeless. Apart from the lack of success of the planes based on Midway, less than fifty of the hundred or so planes from the carriers had found their target, and only seven of them had survived. The Japanese were undoubtedly the more skilful and had far more experience. Six months of uninterrupted success had its value too.

The Japanese had reformed after beating off the attacks, and at 10.20 continued on their northward course in majestic array, the four carriers screened by the two battleships, three cruisers and eleven destroyers. The *Akagi* and *Soryu* were five miles apart and were followed respectively by the *Kaga* and *Hiryu*, two thousand yards astern. On all their flight-decks were aircraft waiting to fly off for the attack scheduled for 10.30.

But first came Lt-Commander McClusky with thirty-seven dive-bombers from the *Enterprise*. They had been airborne since 07.45 and should have turned back to their carrier long before sighting the target, if they were not to risk running out of fuel. But their leader had continued searching for the enemy, and at 09.55 had sighted a Japanese destroyer speeding to the north-east. She had dropped astern of the carriers to attack an American submarine. McClusky took his course from her, and was rewarded by sighting the Japanese formation just after the carriers had been attacked by Massey's torpedo-planes. In spite of the cost to the latter, their attack proved most useful, for when McClusky's bombers went in, the Japanese fighter-planes had not had time to regain height and were not in position to break up the attack.

McClusky split his force; half went screeching down over the *Akagi*, half over the *Kaga*. The former was hit three times; one bomb smashed into the hangar amidships, another split open the flight-deck on the port quarter, and the third burst among the aircraft waiting to fly off. No mortal hurt had been caused – except that in the hangar the bombs which had been left lying about began to explode one after the other. Then the fire spread to the loaded aircraft, and soon the whole hangar was ablaze. Twenty minutes later, Nagumo shifted his flag to the cruiser *Nagara*.

The *Kaga* suffered even more heavily; four hits were scored on her, one blowing the bridge to pieces and another penetrating the hangar and setting fire to bombs and fuel. Soon the carrier was a mass of flames, and the crew began to abandon her. She sank later in the day with a loss of eight hundred men.

Only a few minutes after the *Akagi* and *Kaga* were dealt these mortal blows, a squadron of dive-bombers from the *Yorktown* arrived on the scene and attacked the *Soryu*. They too were fortunate in arriving at a moment when the *Soryu*'s flight-decks had aircraft assembled on them and there was no

LEFT Crew members and pilots examine the damage to USS *Yorktown*; she suffered her death blow on 6 June and sank the following day.

ABOVE A war artist's view of the Japanese carrier fleet at Midway, from left to right the *Akagi*, the *Soryu* and in the foreground the *Kaga*.

BELOW USS *Yorktown* hit by torpedo-carrying bombers from the *Hiryu*.

fighter cover operating. Three hits were obtained with thousand-pound bombs which badly damaged the *Soryu* and set her on fire. The order to abandon ship was given half an hour later.

In a matter of minutes three of the four carriers, the main striking strength of the Japanese fleet, had been eliminated. There remained the *Hiryu*. For the moment she was untouched, well to the north of the other carriers. Her commander flew off his aircraft at 10.30 to make the attack as ordered, and they found the *Yorktown* by following the returning American planes. The fighter cover shot down ten of the Japanese, and anti-aircraft fire accounted for two more, but six bombers got through and obtained three hits which seriously damaged the *Yorktown*. Several fires broke out and her speed dropped to six knots. However, the situation was brought under control and the engineers succeeded in working up a speed of eighteen knots. But the radar and radio were out of service, so Rear-Admiral Fletcher shifted his flag to the cruiser *Astoria*.

The presence of the *Yorktown* was a complete surprise to the Japanese, who believed her to have been sunk at the Battle of the Coral Sea. Nagumo ordered another attack on her, and the *Hiryu* flew off all available aircraft – ten torpedo-carrying bombers, including a survivor from the *Agaki*, and six Zeros, two of which had belonged to the *Kaga*. This force obtained two hits on the *Yorktown*; one torpedo hit her fuel tanks on the port side and another struck her aft, jamming the rudder. She drifted to a stop, and twenty minutes later had a list of twenty-six degrees. At 15.00 her captain gave the order to abandon ship. All her crew of 2,270 were picked up by destroyers in the next two hours.

Meanwhile reconnaissance planes had reported the position of the *Hiryu*: this carrier, two battleships, three cruisers and four destroyers were on a northerly course, 110 miles WNW of the *Yorktown*. Forty-five minutes later, the *Enterprise* turned into the wind and flew off four Douglas bombers for an attack on the remaining enemy carrier – without any fighter escort! The few Wildcats still available were needed as air cover for the fleet. McClusky, the hero of the day, was again in command and his luck stayed with him. In spite of the frantic efforts of the anti-aircraft gunners and although the carrier's commander sent her surging through the water at thirty knots, McClusky and his handful of men scored four hits. The flight-deck was split open and aircraft were set on fire; the engine-room was damaged and cut off by fire from the rest of the ship. The *Hiryu* lost speed. Soon after 21.00 she was lying stopped with a list of fifteen degrees, and it became evident that she was doomed.

Nagumo realized that the situation was hopeless after the *Hiryu* had been put out of action, and he withdrew his force to the northwest. All this time Yamamoto and his battle fleet had been ploughing through a thick mist to the support of his striking force, and the dismal reports received from Nagumo did not make the outlook any brighter. During the evening the blazing and crippled carriers *Soryu* and *Kaga* sank beneath the waves, the former put down by torpedoes from the US submarine *Nautilus*. Yamamoto gave orders for the other two burning carriers to be torpedoed and sunk by destroyers. He knew there were two American carriers still in action; he had only one small carrier with him, and he was still far from the scene of battle. In the small hours of 5 June the Japanese Commander-in-Chief accepted defeat and sent out the order 'Operation Midway is called off . . .'. It had not even continued until D-Day.

The Battle of Midway was a turning point in more senses than one. It marked a change in naval warfare: for all his eleven battleships, Yamamoto had no chance in the face of two undamaged US aircraft-carriers; and it marked the end of Japanese naval predominance in the Pacific, which had lasted a few days short of six months.

Further Reading

Corbett, J. S. *Campaign of Trafalgar*. London, 1910; New York, 1919.

Encyclopedia of Sea Warfare from the First Ironclads to the Present Day. London and New York, 1975.

Hale, J. B. *Famous Sea Fights from Salamis to Jutland*. London, 1939.

Hattersley, Roy. *Nelson*. London and New York, 1974.

Kennedy, Ludovic. *Pursuit: The Sinking of the 'Bismarck'*. London and New York, 1974.

Macintyre, Donald. *Famous Fighting Ships*. London, 1975.

Marcus, G. J. *A Naval History of England*. London, 1961.

Mattingly, Garrett. *The Defeat of the Spanish Armada*. London and Boston, 1959.

Millington-Drake, E. *The Drama of the Graf Spee*. London, 1964.

Mordal, Jacques. *25 Siècles de Guerre sur mer*. Paris, 1959.

Morison, Samuel E. *History of United States Naval Operations in World War II*, 4 volumes. London and Boston, 1949.

Pitt, Barrie. *Coronel and Falkland*. London, 1960.

Thomas, D. A. *Battle of the Java Sea*. London, 1968.

Warner, Oliver. *Nelson and the Age of Fighting Sail*. London, 1963.

Warner, Oliver and Nimitz, Chester W. *Nelson and the Age of Fighting Sail*. New York, 1963.

Warner, Oliver. *Great Battle Fleets*. London, 1971.

Acknowledgments

Photographs and illustrations are supplied by, or reproduced by kind permission of the following:

Australian Ministry of Information: 143 above; Bibliothèque Nationale, Paris: 51, 76 below and below right; Trustees of the British Museum: *10*, *11*, *33 above*; Camera Press: 141 above, 142, 143 below; Cooper-Bridgeman Library: *57 left*, *95 above* and *below*; Coram Foundation: *71*; Ferdinand Urbahns, Eutin: 130; Foto Drüppel, Wilhelmshaven: 107 below, 131; Hachette, Paris: 51; Illustrated London News: 97, 104; Imperial War Museum: 106, 107 above left, 108, 109 above and below, 111, 112 above, 113, 114, 119, 121, 122–3, 125, 126–7, 129 above and below, 131, 132 above and below, 134 above and below, 135 above, 144, 152; Japanese Maritime Self-Defense Force: 99; Keystone Press Agency: 117, 139; Library of Congress: 84 below; Morison History Project: 149; Musée de la Marine, Paris: *66–7*; Museo Navale, Madrid: 28; Museo Storico Navale, Venice: 21, 22; National Maritime Museum: 16, *18–19*, *23*, 26, *31 left* and *right*, *33 below*, 34–5, 35 right, 36 above and *below*, 37, 42, *44–5*, *48 above* and *below*, 50, 52, *53 above* and *below*, *57 right* and *left*, *60*, *61*, 63 above and below, 68, *70 below*, 72–3, 77, *78–9*, *82*, *86 above* and *below*, 88, *91 above* and *below*, 92, *107 above right*, *110*, 112 below, *151*; National Portrait Gallery: 29; Naval Historical Section, Royal Netherlands Navy: 138, 141 below; Nelson Museum, Monmouth: 62, 64; Novosti Press Agency: 101; Paul Elek Archives: *11*; Picturepoint: 26, *33 below*, *78–9*, *90*, *102 above* and *below*; Popperfoto: 135 below, 146, 147 below; Radio Times Hulton Picture Library: 12, 13, 17, 20, 38, 41 above and below, 43, 54, 55, 59 below, 76 above left, above right and below left, 80, 84 above, 87, 89 above and below, 93, 98 below, 100, 105, 118 above; Science Museum, London: 25–6, 118 below, 147 above; Shizuo Fukui: 98 above left and above right; Tate Gallery: *70 above*; US Navy/National Archives, Washington: 148, 153, *154 above* and below; Palace of Versailles: *49*; Victoria and Albert Museum: 59 above, *95 above* and *below*; Weidenfeld and Nicolson Archives: *30*.

Numbers and directions in italics refer to colour illustrations.

Maps drawn by D. P. Press.

Index

Achilles, 118–22
Agrippine, 89
Aigle, 71
Ajax (1781), 51
Ajax (1939), 118, *118*, 119–20, 122
Akagi, 150, 152–3, *154*, 155
Alabama, 89, 90, *90*, 92, *92*, 93, *93*
Albion, 81
Algesiras, 71
Ali, El Louck, 20, 26–7
Ali, Mehemet, 75
Ali Pasha, 15, 20–3
Alliance, 40–1, *42*, 46
Ark Royal, 118, 133–4, 136
Asia, 76, 80
Astoria, 154
Auguste, 51
Azores, 89, 133

Baltic Sea, 94, 125
Barbarigo, Agostino, 16, 20–1, *21*, 22
Barbavera, Captain, 9–12, 14
Barfleur, 49
Barham, First Sea Lord, 60–1
Barras de St Laurent, 48–9, 51
Batavia, 144–5
Bay of Biscay, 22, 59
Béhuchet, Nicolas, 11, 14
Bell, Captain, 119
Berwick, 71
Biedovy, 104
Bismarck, 125, *125*, 128, 130–1, *131*, 133–4, 136
Blenheim, 58
Bonhomme Richard see *Poor Richard*
Borodino, 101, 103
Brest, 47, 59, 133, 136
Bristol, 105
Bucentaure, 65, 71, 74
Buchanan, Captain, 83, 85, 87–8
Buiny, 102, 104

Cadiz, 52, 59–60, 62, 64–5, 74
Calais Roads, 33
Calder, Sir Robert, 60
Camperdown, 52
Canning, George, 75
Canopus, 107
Cape Finisterre, 28, 60, 74

Captain, 52, *54*, 55, 58
Carnavon, 105, *109*, 110–11
Caton, 51
Cherbourg, 14, 89, 93
Chesapeake Bay, 48, *48*, 49, *49*, 51, 83, 85
Clement, 115
Cochrane, Lord, 76, *76*
Codrington, Vice-Admiral Sir Edward, 75, 76, *76*, 80, 82
Collingwood, Admiral Lord, 54, 61, 65, 68, 71, 74
Concorde, 48
Congress, 85, 87
Conqueror, 71, 74
Cordoba, Admiral, 58
Corfu, 16, 17, 20
Cornwall, 105, 108, 110, 112–13
Cornwallis, Lord, 49, 51, 59–60, 61
Coronel, 105–6, *106*, 110
Cossack, 136
Countess of Scarborough, 41, 46
Culloden, 54, 58
Cumberland (1862), 85, 87, *87*, 88
Cumberland (1939), 120, 124
Curious, 59–60

d'Andrada, Gil, 17
Daphne, 81
Dartmouth, 80
Davis, President of Confederate States of America, 89
de Bougainville, Louis-Antoine, 51, *51*
de Cardona, Juan, 16
Deerhound, 90, 93, *93*
Defiance, 71
de Grasse, Admiral François, 47, 48, *48*, 49, 51
de Heyden, Rear-Admiral Count, 75, 76
R. Delaware, 85
de Rigny, Rear-Admiral Gauthier, 75, 76, 80, 82
De Ruyter, 137–8, *138*, 142
d'Estelang, Pierre, 14
Dewa, Rear-Admiral, 101
Diadème, 51
Doorman, Rear-Admiral Karel, 137–42

Don John of Austria, 15–17, *17*, 20–3, 26–7
Doria, Andrea, 16, *20*, 21, 23, 26–7
Doric Star, 115
Dorsetshire, *134*, 136
Drake, Sir Francis, *17*, 30, 32, *33*, 34–5
Drake, Samuel Francis, 49–51
Drake, 40
Dresden, 105, 110, 112, 114
Drummuir, 107
Duc de Duras, 40
Dumanoir, Rear-Admiral, 68, 74
Duncan, Admiral Adam, 52

Edinburgh, 133
Edward III, King of England, 9, *10*, 11, 14
Electra, 138–9, 141
Elizabeth I of England, *30*
Encounter, 138, 142, 144–5
Enterprise, 146, 150–2, 155
Excellent, 54, 58
Exeter, 118–19, 138, 139, *139*, 140–1, 144, 145, *145*

Falkland Islands, 105–8, 120
Fisher, Admiral Lord, 105, 114
Flanders, 9, 14, 32, 37
Fleming, Captain Thomas, 30, 32
Fletcher, Rear-Admiral Frank Jack, 148, *148*, 150, 154
Flores de Valdes, Diego, 28
Folkersham, Rear-Admiral, 96, 102
Fougueux, 71, 74
Froissart, Jean, 9, *11*
Fuji, 103

Ganteaume, Vice-Admiral, 59, 61
Gibraltar, 59, 74
Glasgow, 105, 108, *109*, 110, 112–14
Gneisenau, 105–6, *107*, 108, 110–11, *112*, 125
Golden Hind, 28
Goldsborough, Admiral, 85
Gordon, Captain Oliver, 138, 140, 145
(*Admiral*) *Graf Spee*, 115, 118, *118*, 119, *119*, 120–1, *121*, 122, *122*, 123–4

Graves, Rear-Admiral Sir Thomas, 48, 50, *50*, 51
Gravina, Admiral, 59, 64
Great Christopher, 10, 12
Gulf of Patras, 15, 17, 76

Hague Convention, 121, 123
Haguro, 139, 142, 145
Hampton Roads, 48-9, 87, *87*
Harris, Captain, 115
Harwood, Commodore (later Rear-Admiral) Henry, 118, *118*, 119, 120-1, 123-4
Hawkins, John, 32, 34, *35*
Helfrich, Vice-Admiral C., 137-8, 141
Hiryu, 152-3, 155
Holland, Vice-Admiral L., 128, 130
Holy League, 15
Hood, Rear-Admiral Sir Samuel, 47-51, 64
Hood, 125, 128, 130-1, *131*, 134
Hornet, 146, 150, *151*, *152*
Houston, 138-42, *143*, 145
Howard of Effingham, Lord Admiral Charles, 28, *31*, 31-2, 34-5, 37
R. Hudson, 48-9

Ibrahim Pasha, 75-6, *76*, 80, 82
Imperator Alexander III, 100, *101*
Imperator Nikolai I, 98, 103
Indian Ocean, 96, 144
Indomitable, 74
Inflexible, 105, 110-11, *112*
Intrepid, 51
Invincible, 105, 110, *111*, 112
Irania, 81-2
Irish Sea, 40
Izumrud, 103

Java, 137, 141-2
Java, 138, 142
Jellicoe, Sir John, 105, *105*
Jervis, Admiral Sir John, 52, *52*, 54, 58
Jintsu, 139, *141*
Jones, Lieutenant, 87-8
Jones, John Paul, 40, *41*, 43, 46
Julian calendar, 28
Jupiter, 138-9, 142, *142*

Kaga, 150, 152-3, *154*, 155
Kearsage, 90, *90*, 92-3
Kell, First Lieutenant John McIntosh, 89, *89*, 93
Kent, 105, 110, 112-13, *113*, 114, *114*
Khodja, Kara, 15, 20
King George V, 125, 131, 133, *134*, 136

Knias Souvaroff, 94, 100-1, 103
Knights of Malta, 15, 26
Kortenaer, 140, 142

Lancaster, John, 93
Landais, Pierre, 40, *42*, 46
Langsdorff, Kapitan zur See Hans, 115, 118, 120-1, 124
Leach, Captain John, *129*, 131
Le Havre, 32, 89
Leipzig, 105, 107, 110, 112-13
Lindemann, Captain Ernst, 125, 136
London (1781), 49, 51
London (1939), 133
Luce, Captain, 105, 112-13
Lütjens, Admiral Günther, 125, *125*, 130-1, 133

McCluskey, Lt-Commander, 152-3, 155
Magon, Rear-Admiral, 71
Mars, 71
Massey, Lt-Commander, 151, 153
Medina Sidonia, Duke of, 28, *28*, 32-3, 37-9
Merrimack see *Virginia*
Messina, 15, 20, 27
Mikasa, 98, *99*, 100, *104*
Minnesota, 85, 87-8
Monarca, 71
Monitor, 83, *84*, 85, 87, *87*, 88
Montevideo, 120-1, *121*, 123-4

Nachi, 139-40, 142, 145
Nagara, 153
Nagumo, Vice-Admiral, 146, 149, *149*, 150, 153, 155
Napoleon, 59, *59*, 61-2, 74
Nautilus, 155
Navarin, 103
Nebogatoff, Rear-Admiral, 97, *97*, 102-3
Nelson, Admiral Lord, 52, 54, *54*, 55, *55*, 57, 58, 60, *60*, 62, *62*, 64, *64*, 65, 68, *68*
Neptuno, 74
Nimitz, Admiral Chester, 146, *147*, 149
Norfolk, 125, 128, 130-1, *133*, 136
North Sea, 33, 37, 125
Nuestra Señora del Rosario, 32, *33*
Nürnberg, 105, 106, *107*, 108, 110, 112-14, *114*

Orel, 98, 103
Ossliabya, 100

Pallas, 40-1, 46
Parma, Duke of, 28, 32-4, 37
Pearson, Captain Richard, 40-1, *41*, 43, 46

Perth, 138, 140, 142, *143*, 145
Petrona Bey, 76
Philip II, King of Spain, 28, *29*, 39
Philippe VI (Philippe of Valois), King of France, 9, *10*, 14
Pius V, Pope, 15, *16*
R. Plate, 118-22
Plymouth, 28, 30, *33*, 74
Poor Richard, 40, 41, *42*, 46
Pope, 144-5
Port Arthur, 94, 96, 104
Port Stanley, 106-8, 113-14
Prince of Wales, 125, 128, *129*, 130-1, 133
Princessa, 49, 51
Principe de Asturias, 74
Prinz Eugen, 125, 128, *129*, 130, *130*, 131, 136
Pylos, 76

Quiéret, Admiral Hue, 9-12, 14

Ranger, 40
Reale, *16*, 20-3
Redoutable, 65, *65*, 71, 74
Refléchi, 51
Renown, 118, 133-4
Repulse, 125, 131
Revenge, 32, *33*
Roanoke, 85
Rochambeau, General, 47-8, 51
Rodney, Admiral Lord, 51
Rodney, 133, *134*, 136
Rojestvensky, Admiral Sinovie Petrovitch, 94, 96-102, 104
Royal Sovereign, 65, 71

St Esprit, 51
St George, 10-11, 14
St Lawrence, 85
San Bahama, 74
San Idelfonso, 74
San Josef, 55, 58
San Juan Nepomuceno, 74
San Lorenzo, 35
San Martin, 28, 38-9
San Nicholas, 52, 54, 55, 58
San Salvador, 32
Santa Anna, 65, 71
Santa Cruz, Marquis of, *16*, 27
Santissima Trinidad, 52, 58, 71
Scapa Flow, 125, 130
Scharnhorst, 105, 106, *106*, 108, 110-11, 125
Scheldt estuary, 9-10
Scipion, 81
Scirocco, Mohammed, 20-2
Sea of Japan, 103-4
Semmes, Captain Raphael (Old Beeswax), 89, *89*, 90, 92-3

Serapis, 40-1, *41*, *42*, *43*, 46
Seymour, Lord, 33
Sheffield, 133-4, 136
Shrewsbury, 51
Sirène, 80-2
Sirius, 64
Somerville, Vice-Admiral Sir James, 133-4, 136
Soryu, 151-3, *154*, 155
Sourabaya, 137-8, 141-2, 144-5
Starr, Captain, 118
Stirling, Captain, 59
Stoddart, Rear-Admiral A. P., 105, *108*, 110
Strachan, Commodore, 74
Sturdee, Vice-Admiral Sir Frederick Doveton, 105-7, *107*, 108, 110, 112, 114
Suffolk, 125, 128, 130-1, 133, *133*
Sultan of Morocco, 96
Sumter, 89
Svietlana, 101
Swallow, 48
Swiftsure, 71, 74

Tacoma, 124
Tairoa, 115, 118
Takagi, Admiral, 140
Tangiers, 96
Temeraire, 68, 71
Terrible, 51
Thames estuary, 9, 37
Thomas, 9-10, 14
Togo, Admiral, 98, *98*, 99-101, 103, *104*
Toulon, 59, 64, 74
Tovey, Admiral, 125, *129*, 131, 133-4, 136
Trident, 82
Tristan da Cunha, 115
Troubridge, Captain Thomas, 54

Uriu, Captain, 101

Vengeance, 40
Vian, Captain, 136
Victorious, 125, 131, 133
Victory, *52*, 61-2, 64, *64*, 68, 71
Villeneuve, Vice-Admiral Pierre, 59, *59*, 60, 62, 64, 71, 74

Virginia, 83, 85, 87, *87*, 88
Vladivostock, 94, 98-9, 102-4
Von Spee, Vice-Admiral Graf, 105-7, 110-11, *110*, *112*

Waldron, Lt-Commander John C., 150
Waller, Captain, 142
Washbourn, Lieutenant (later Rear-Admiral), 121
Washington, General George, 47-9, 51
West Indies, 47, 59
Wight, Isle of, 32, *36*
Winslow, Captain John, 90, 92-3
Witte de With, 141, *141*, 144-5
Worden, Lt-Commander John L., 83, 88

Yamamoto, Admiral, 146, *146*
Yamoto, 146, *147*, 155
Yorktown, 49, 51
Yorktown, 146, 148, 151, 153, *153*, 154, *154*, 155